THE CYCLIST'S MANIFESTO

THE CYCLIST'S MANIFESTO

The Case for Riding on Two Wheels Instead of Four

ROBERT HURST

FALCONGUIDES ®

Guilford, Connecticut
Helena, Montana
An imprint of The Globe Pequot Press

FALCONGUIDES

Copyright © 2009 Robert Hurst

Text designer: Libby Kingsbury
Layout artist: Kim Burdick
Project manager: John Burbidge

Library of Congress Cataloging-in-Publication Data

Hurst, Robert (Robert J.)
  Cyclist's manifesto : the case for riding on two wheels instead of four / Robert
Hurst.
     p. cm.
  Includes bibliographical references and index.
  ISBN 978-0-7627-5128-0
  1. Cycling—Social aspects. 2. Cyclists. I. Title.
  GV1043.7.H883 2009
  796.6—dc22
                                    2009005027

Printed in the United States of America
10 9 8 7 6 5 4 3 2

To Christie, with whom I am always trying to keep up

Contents

INTERESTING TIMES

Of Explosions and Implosions

A DULL ROAR, AMONG OTHER THINGS, WAFTS THROUGH THE open window here, 24-7. The freeway is about a half mile away, alternately hissing, whispering, and humming with the sound of tires on pavement. Traffic streams along I-25 day and night, and from here it actually sounds a bit like a mountain river, fourteen lanes wide. A high-pitched sport bike speeds off into the distance, dominating the avant-garde symphony for a few moments. I visualize its pilot hunched down over the gas tank, ecstatic. A Harley takes off after it in a clatter of explosions. The steady *tch-tch tch-tch* and baritone rumble of coal trains slow-chugging through the BN & SF rail yard under the highway every twenty minutes. Jets headed west over the Rockies, Pratt & Whitneys broadcasting proudly across miles of sky. And the helicopters buzzing from horizon to horizon. The military versions are instantly recognizable by the extra *whup-whup-whup* of their special wide blades—the guys who figured that it was a good idea to rely so heavily on these things in guerrilla wars, and *whup-whup-whup* exact troop locations to anyone within ten miles, were perhaps not thinking straight. But I didn't go to war college.

Those wondering what society is all about could get some ideas just by listening to it. It sounds like explosions encased in steel. Citizens of this clattering, heavily motorized world are slurping up about eighty-five million barrels of liquid petroleum every day and exploding the vast majority of it inside the combustion chambers of their motor vehicles. This number is down a bit from the all-time high (reached sometime around January 2008) as a worldwide economic slump has weighed heavily on habits of petroleum consumption around the globe. This decline in oil consumption was the first in the United States—where 5 percent of the world's population consumes a quarter of its oil—in more than twenty years, and thus a real eyebrow-raiser.

The price of oil and the pace of economic activity affect each other in myriad and complex ways, a continuous feedback loop. There is no beginning or end to it, so it is folly to try to sort out cause and effect in these markets. Some of the causes are effects and some of the effects moonlight as causes. It should be noted, however, that ten of the last eleven recessions were immediately preceded by spikes in the price of oil. It doesn't mean that the oil spikes caused the recessions, but it sure doesn't mean they didn't.

Sometime during the summer of 2008, I walked past two women having a conversation on the sidewalk downtown. They were dressed smartly and appeared to be two successful professionals. I caught just enough of their conversation to get that one was explaining to the other, in step-by-step detail, how to siphon gas. Interesting times. The price of crude topped $100 in January, shot up to $147, contrary to expectations, and then, just as soon as most people lost their cookies and started to predict an assault on $200, fell $90 in ninety days with the flappy sound of a whoopee cushion. It has been, by far, the most insane year the energy markets have ever seen. Completely unprecedented. As the summer of 2008 turned to fall, the oil situation continued in such volatility, such uncertainty, such along-for-the-ride-ness, that at this point the price of crude could spike back to $150 or sink into the single digits and the top experts and energy consultants would just shrug it off. Whatcha gonna do? They lost their handle on this thing a long time ago. The energy markets became an uncontrolled fire hose, blasting this way and that at high pressure, and seemingly in chaos. Analysts of the Peak Oil persuasion predicted tremendous, unprecedented volatility as a consequence of a plateau in global oil production, and economic chaos as a consequence of a spike in oil futures; their ideological foes among the economists contended that supply issues were illusory and said the price of oil would collapse to its familiar low level. The world-wide economic disaster of 2008 gave both groups a chance to appear correct for a while, but nobody can say with any authority which way(s) the oil market will go in the next six months or a year.

It's a crazy time to write a book relating to energy, as it's all happening right now. While nobody can predict the future of energy with much certainty, because there isn't enough reliable information available and the price per barrel travels in both directions with conviction, and the commodities markets could very well be manipulated by nefarious forces, I believe our energy future is starting to reveal itself. Evidence is now convincing that the world has already entered a new phase in its energy history—a phase that promises to be relentlessly interesting.

The Invisible Solution

The high point of his campaign, so far, has been his energy policy, which is comprehensive and bold, but does not try to turn us into a nation of bicyclists.

David Brooks, referring to presidential candidate John McCain in the *New York Times,* July 2008[1]

I know there are bicyclists out there, and in increasing numbers, but I can't hear them. Bicyclists don't broadcast their movements for the entire jungle or the entire city.

As you may have guessed by the title of this thing, I'm here to promote the bicycle. But I'll put this out there right at the start: The bicycle is not going to solve our energy problems. The bicycle is not going to make the United States independent of foreign oil. And the United States is not going to morph into a nation of bicyclists as it does in the darkest apocalyptic visions of David Brooks. The first thing we need is for people to be realistic.

As the energy monster emerges from the shadows and starts to reveal the furry edges of itself to a sleepy populace,

Americans cling with renewed urgency to the ideal of the personal automobile. Sure, Americans drive less as energy prices rise, but most of us are driving a little less while looking forward to the plug-in electrics, the theoretical hydrogen and compressed-air cars that will surely bring back the days of driving with impunity. In these popular visions of the future, technology comes riding to the rescue of the American Way of Life, and the thought of having to drive less is exiled to the back alleys of the mind. The simplest solutions—those that don't involve carrying a few tons of metal and plastic around everywhere we go—are banished from the discussion. It's a colossal and perhaps fatal failure of imagination.

In the public realm, the notion of bicycling for transportation, when mentioned at all, still tends to be treated as some sort of joke. On the radar screens of the officials and technocrats charged with figuring all this out, bicycling registers scarcely a blip. For instance, a commission appointed by the Department of Commerce prepared a highly touted report for President-elect Obama and Congress in 2008: "A Transition Plan for America's Energy Future." The report contained no fewer than eighty-eight separate recommendations. Some were good, and some, like the continued subsidization of ethanol, were very bad. In typical fashion, the plan included not a single word about human-powered transport. Observing all this, I am under no illusions that bicycling will become a primary mode of everyday transportation in this country. We are all-in for driving. David Brooks will continue to be chauffered around Washington and Manhattan in the back of a Lincoln Town Car for the foreseeable future. At some point he may switch to a hybrid Lincoln Town Car.

Many serious analysts—and a lot of shysters too—agree that there is no single solution to the energy challenges of the twenty-first century. If we are ever going to halt the heinous and massive transfer of American wealth to hostile or indifferent, undemocratic "petro-states," if it is somehow possible to lift ourselves off the hook of dependence, a multi-pronged response will be necessary, with many sources and strategies put to work at the same time. I believe the bicycle could, and should, become one component of this multifaceted solution.

There are a lot of easy things that can be done to get us moving in that direction, and I'll mention a few of them along the way. But the bicycle works its real magic on the level of the individual. The bicycle won't solve the world's problems. That rocket has launched. It could very well solve some of yours, however. On an individual level the bicycle transforms lives, in times of plenty and times of hardship. I may be able to convince some readers of these things eventually. First, let's look back and see if we can figure out what in the hell happened.

CIRCLE OF POWER

Night Dreams

It began with the bicycle. Summer, 1892. A young Hiram Percy Maxim,* superintendent of a bullet factory in West Lynn, Massachusetts, was pedaling back home from Salem in the dead of night. Salem and Lynn were connected by about five miles of dark road. Maxim enjoyed riding his bicycle but on this particular night, after a notably successful date, he found himself running on empty and wishing he didn't have to pedal anymore. But there he was, dangling out there on old Essex Road and detecting his proximity to the Swampscott Cemetery by its earthy smell. At this moment of grumbling dissatisfaction with his mode of travel, the little mustachioed MIT grad looked down at the cranks and

---

*Hiram Percy Maxim was the son of Hiram Stevens Maxim, inventor of the fully automatic Maxim gun. The younger Maxim, after developing the vehicles discussed here, became known for inventing the silencer, without which the television show *Mission: Impossible* would never have been created.

bottom bracket and the pedals inexorably turning—the Circle of Power of his fixed-wheel machine—and experienced a flash of inspiration. I might be able to attach a small gasoline engine to this thing and dispense with the pedaling. Even better, his thought progressed—or devolved, as the case may be—I could put a gas engine on a buggy and dispense with the bicycle altogether. Maxim imagined pushing a button or pulling a lever and being spirited away to his doorstep as if by magic, without physical effort. We can do this, he thought. He went into a happy trance while rolling through the darkened farmland. Instead of watching the road ahead, he gazed into the future of human transport and saw bicycles, horses, and trains all bludgeoned into obsolescence by motorization.[1] Good thing he didn't hit any potholes while trancing out in the dark, or he would have eaten some of that road between Salem and Lynn.

Lately, the Massachusetts Highway Department is reporting that the flow rate along Maxim's old route is in the neighborhood of twenty-five thousand motorized vehicles per day. The hallucination has become real. The world has been Maxim-ized.

The Bicycle Idea

Maxim's idea will seem quite ordinary to us today, but it bordered on revolutionary in 1892, when the rare seeker of gasoline had to acquire the stuff in eight-ounce increments from highly suspicious paint store clerks. Given the relative scarcity of small gasoline engines at that time, and the fact that he had never in his life seen one attached to a bicycle or carriage, Maxim figured his Aha! moment might have been original and highly consequential. He later found out that many others around the world had already been visited by similar thoughts. Motor-carriages were in commercial production in France in the early 1890s.[2] In the United States, Maxim's lightning bolt of inspiration was just one of many; similar bolts smacked George Selden, H. K. Shanck, Alexander Winton, Elwood Haynes, Charles King, Henry Ford, Ransom Olds, and the Duryea brothers, most notably, and no doubt many others. Winton and Shanck were each building bicycles in Ohio when their inspiration hit, years apart. The Duryeas, who were the first Americans to build a gas-powered car that actually functioned, were bike mechanics and bike manufacturers when they accomplished the feat.[3]

Many decades later Maxim offered a theory to explain why so many different engineers, machinists, and tinkers fell under the influence of the Motor Madness at nearly the same time, each substantially ignorant of the others' efforts:

> We have had the steam-engine for over a century. We could have built steam vehicles in 1880, or indeed in 1870. But we did not. We waited until 1895.
>
> The reason why we did not build mechanical road vehicles before this, in my opinion, was because the bicycle had not yet come in numbers and had not directed men's minds to the possibilities of independent, long-distance

travel over the ordinary highway. We thought the railroad was good enough. The bicycle created a new demand which it was beyond the ability of the railroads to supply. Then it came about that the bicycle could not satisfy the demand which it had created.[4]

This passage has been quoted often, and Maxim's theory endorsed by many scholars of automotive history. That doesn't mean he's right, of course. There may be some holes in the theory. For instance, it's not true that steam-powered vehicles weren't produced prior to the bicycle craze. They were, although without much success. But Maxim was right there in the thick of things, so his opinion carries the weight of personal experience along with its simple elegance. The bicycle, particularly the modern-style "safety bicycle" with pneumatic tires, gave people this delicious and unprecedented taste of freedom, an awakening to the possibilities of a different kind of travel altogether after thousands of years of draft animals hauling wagons. Quite a bite of apple that was. Suddenly everyone could see the possibility of using machines to roll freely over the roads for long distances, at any time of their choosing, at twice the speed of a horse. Thus with a pedal stroke it vanquished foot travel, horse travel, train travel— and bicycle travel, too.

It's safe to say that some riders in Maxim's day took from their bicycles great rewards that were separate and distinct from mere transportation. While moving from here to there with unprecedented efficiency, they also reveled in the exhilaration of speed and balance peculiar to an in-line two-wheel vehicle. Rather than being chased into the arms of motors by the thought of the physical exertion required to propel the "bike-rider system," some enjoyed that part of bicycling, too. To these riders no greater form of transport needed to be invented. The bike was their dream, realized—the bike was the realization of a dream they hadn't even dreamed yet.

But to some others, it just left them hanging out there on the road between Salem and Lynn, wanting more. To Maxim, et al., the bicycle was a puzzle that demanded a solution.

Maxim, Pope, and the LAW

Maxim was transformed by his vision and could think of little but gasoline engines and mythical motorcars for several years. He became useless at the bullet factory and began to exhibit symptoms usually seen in the later stages of human-to-werewolf transformation. Having heard of a small engine driving a water pump somewhere nearby, he went to see it at first opportunity, brimming with excitement. It seems likely that he may have been foaming at the mouth a bit as he stared at the motor long and hard, caressed it, listened to it, fell in love. Maxim was simply obsessed with the thought of driving a magic motorcar, and he was not alone.

In the following year he designed and pieced together his own engine, then mounted it on a rickety tandem tricycle. The contraption was a flop as a practical vehicle, struggling to manage walking speed up slight grades and toppling over with frightening ease. Unsafe at any speed. Even so, his machine was a mindblower. Maxim's experiments soon attracted attention from higher-ups at the Pope Manufacturing Company. Pope was then the leading producer of bicycles in the United States, with thousands of employees and five factories[5]—in fact, the tricycle upon which Maxim placed his first engine was a Pope Company product.

Maxim became chief engineer of the newly formed Pope Motor-carriage Division.

Colonel Albert Pope, the man behind the Pope Company, had been America's first and most successful bicycle maker, but also its first major cycling advocate. In 1880, during the high-wheeler era, he created the League of American Wheelmen (LAW). Although his first thought was probably for marketing his Columbia-brand bicycles, the League grew into a multi-pronged organization with impressive reach into wide-ranging aspects of bicycling. It served cycle tourists with maps and guides, sparred with a natural enemy in the railroads, and pestered lawmakers into a variety of bicyclist-friendly provisions. It even wrested control of the racing side of things, which was big business. It is inconceivable to imagine one of today's broad-based cycling advocacy organizations (like the League of American Bicyclists, the LAW's post-post-modern successor) with its fingers in the racing cookie jar.

Most notably, the LAW succeeded in a widespread movement to have public roads paved and improved, primarily to benefit recreational bicyclists (and the bicycle industry). The League was not an order of utility cyclists, mind you, trying to improve their routes to work. These were primarily weekend warriors, coming at the politicians in such numbers and with such combativeness that the politicians couldn't resist. Their Good Roads Movement altered the landscape noticeably, changed the country's expectations about street surfaces, and benefited the early auto builders in obvious ways.

The bleating of the Wheelmen improved the infrastructure and institutional framework for bicyclists—for road transportation in general. It even laid the foundation for bicyclists' basic legal right to use the roadways, which, if you're a bicyclist or thinking of becoming one, is critically important. But the bitter fights over things like road paving, access to Central Park, and whether bicyclists should be allowed to take their wheels aboard trains for free must have seemed pretty silly to the wider population. Complaints rang hollow when the complainers used their bicycles almost exclusively as toys and otherwise lived their lives in conspicuous comfort. Still, the LAW cried discrimination and made lists of "targeted" politicians whenever they met resistance to their demands. They won many of these scraps. In the process they may have given the well-to-do wheelmen a reputation for insufferable spoiled whining. Bicyclists have had a hard time shaking this rap, partly because it's been a convenient narrative for anti-bicycle forces, and partly because it's true.

By 1898 Colonel Pope's company, thanks in large part to Hiram Percy Maxim, was selling a variety of reliable self-propelled four-wheel vehicles, both electric and gas powered. That year the League saw its enrollment contract for the first time, dropping 15 percent in six months.[6] Within a few decades the LAW would drop off the map, along with interest in bicycling among adults in the United States.

To Be Taken Seriously

Eighteen ninety-three was a great year for the bike industry but perhaps not so great for the bike. Big cities around the world were experiencing large increases in the numbers of bicyclists on the streets and an even more pronounced increase in the numbers of unscrupulous or reckless riders, setting the stage for conflict and contempt. In New York City anger toward bicyclists erupted when one Edward Kleinschmidt ran over and killed a little girl named Katie McGlynn on May 26. The tragedy set the tone for the rest of the summer. Pedestrians and cart drivers intensified their hateful glaring at the growing crowd of bicyclists. The *New York Times* editorialized in favor of registration, licensing, and greater enforcement applied to wheel jockeys—all of which echoes perfectly in contemporary arguments.

The bicyclists glared at each other in distrust as well. Isaac Potter, a well-known cycling advocate of his day, was quoted in the *Times* denouncing the new crop of rolling hoodlums, seeking to draw a distinction between the unsavory newcomers and the "respectable" old-school wheelmen.

Years before the death of Katie McGlynn, Potter had been instrumental in the passage of a New York state law granting bicyclists all the rights and responsibilities of vehicles— vehicles meaning horse-drawn carriages. Carriages were then limited by law to a maximum speed of five miles per hour in New York. Obviously, it was easy to pedal a bike at more than three times this speed; it was also easy to use a bicycle in places and in ways a carriage could not operate, and many wheelmen did exactly that. The NYC police in the early 1890s did not feel particularly threatened by this new brand of lawbreaking and settled into a hands-off policy, ignoring the classification of bicycles as carriages and allowing bicyclists the freedom of movement inherent in their machines. With the public outcry over the girl's death amid growing traffic chaos, the police launched a bit of a crackdown on speeders—one of the first of dozens of crackdowns against scofflaw bicyclists that would be launched in cities throughout North America over the next century—and outfitted the first bicycle cops for the specific purpose of chasing down other bicyclists.[7]

But let's go back—why would Isaac Potter or anyone who rides a bike want to be classified with carriages? Given the maneuverability and potential speed of bicycles, isn't that a big step down? At the time Potter wrote this law and pushed it through, 1887, the wheelmen had been banned from Central Park, one of the best places to ride. The new law was a compromise of sorts that placed bicyclists under far greater control of the Man, but guaranteed their right to travel wherever other vehicles were allowed to go. Thus the wheels would not be banished from the park or any other public road. This was viewed as a major victory by many New York wheelmen, and they dubbed it "The Liberty Law."[8]

Some wheelmen did not appreciate the sweeping and sudden criminalization of many of the new safety bicycle's advantages. If there was a third way, perhaps to create laws that would be more accommodating of the bicycle's unique capabilities, such an alternative seems never to have been considered.

To Potter and his ilk, the compromise of holding bicyclists to vehicular laws while guaranteeing them vehicular rights was well worth it. In fact, it wasn't viewed as much of a compromise at all. One gets the impression that the Potters yearned to roll at five miles per hour in the most deliberate carriage-like fashion, law or not. Anybody riding like that could hardly be accused of using their bicycle as a toy. Above all else Potter and his like-minded wheelmen yearned to be taken seriously.

Gapers

In 1895, after numerous test runs around the company yard, Maxim took his first halting drive through the streets of Hartford in his prototype Pope gasoline-powered horseless carriage. His assistant rode alongside on a bicycle with a sack of tools and spare parts, fully expecting a breakdown. Maxim didn't appreciate audiences for his experiments, so he was unsettled when a procession of an additional twenty to thirty bicyclists formed behind—random strangers seeming to accumulate like moths around a porch light. This would become a familiar but disconcerting routine. Maxim wrote, "It should be remembered that I never took the machine out that I did not collect a flock of bicyclists who followed me around as children follow a parade."[9]

Horses displayed nearly the opposite reaction. Every time Maxim encountered a horse on the roadways while driving his carriage, he had to stop, dismount, glide over to soothe the animal, and lead it past the car. When he failed to perform this ritual in time, the horses panicked, reared up, and occasionally, if they were good country horses, tried to stomp his clattering alien machine into submission. Dealing with horses and bicyclists was among Maxim's least favorite aspects of being a transportation visionary.

Not Enough

It's not enough to say that the bicycle planted the dream of a certain type of mobility in the human psyche; the booming bicycle business of the early 1890s also made fulfillment of that dream possible in direct ways, spawning multiple industrial advances that were needed by the automakers in ensuing years. Bike tech created ball bearings, frames constructed from hollow welded steel tubes, lighter and stronger alloys, spoked wheels, mastery of chains and gears, and, crucially, pneumatic tires, all of which showed up in the first cars. Also, of course, the specialized tools needed to make all these things. Add to the list of contributions, simply, manpower—the bike manufacturers became carmakers. Their ideas for running factories and marketing their products and creatively bilking their customers were transferred to a new industry. Even the bike racers got into the act, abandoning the wooden tracks in droves to build and drive race cars.

It would be difficult to overstate the influence of the bicycle on the ensuing motor age. But I might try anyway—watch out.

Ford Gawks King

Inventor, n. A person who makes an ingenious arrangement of wheels, levers and springs, and believes it civilization.

Ambrose Bierce, *The Devil's Dictionary*[10]

On March 6, 1896, Charles King, one of the important pioneers whose name has been almost lost to history, exhibited his motorized wagon in Detroit. He showed off a top speed of eight miles per hour—definitely goggle-worthy. Everybody hold on tight.

A flock of bicyclists quickly materialized, swarming the novel machine as it chugged around in a cloud of exhaust and noise. Our old bud Henry Ford was pedaling with the peanut gallery that day. He was gathering intelligence for his own effort, the "Quadricycle," which was brewing in his garage a short distance away.[11]

Ford's Quadricycle was finished and ready to roll just a few months after King's exhibition. At this point Ford learned that the shed door wasn't as wide as the completed vehicle, so he grabbed a blunt instrument and bashed out the bricks on one side (he was renting) to get the thing out. At about three in the morning on June 4, 1896, Ford and a distinguished few mechanics birthed from the altered structure a five-hundred-pound gasoline-powered contraption that had four bicycle wheels, a frame of steel bicycle tubing, and a bicycle seat.[12]

E. G. Graham was one of many who received a ride in the Quadricycle that summer.

> I recollect there was quite a cloud of smoke well in the air behind us, and we hadn't gone far before there were twenty-five to fifty bicyclists following us. We circled around—I do not remember where—until finally we reached Lafayette Street, going west, and when we got fairly close to Fourth Street Mr. Ford instructed me when we turned the corner to jump out and run and open the door of the stable so that the car could be driven in before the crowd of bicyclists overtook us. This was done, and Mr. Ford had just snapped the padlock in the hasp when around the corner they came and one of them said, "Mister, can you tell us where that horseless carriage went?" Henry replied, "Yes, right up that alley," and away they went up the alley to the east. Mr. Ford gave one of his humorous chuckles, and we walked back to the Edison station.[13]

The wheelmen seemed hypnotized by these early motorcars. When they saw or heard one, or heard of one, they took leave of their senses, like paparazzi chasing Brad Pitt. They went to the machine as if to a mother ship or queen bee.

Flight

Back in the day, if you wanted to buy a bike in Boulder, Colorado—one of the country's all-time iconic bicycle-oriented communities—you went to see Eddie Kiefer. Business was strong at Kiefer's downtown shop in the early 1890s. Seemed like everybody wanted a Walther pneumatic and he couldn't keep enough in stock. But 1895 seems to be the year that the bike biz jumped the shark in Boulder. Sales started strong that summer, then ended with a fizzle.

On the first of December, 1895, Kiefer told his lone employee that he was off to the nearby hamlet of Marshall to trade a bicycle. A ride in Boulder in December can be miserable, or positively glorious. That day was one of the great ones: clear blue sky, crisp cold air, and a dusting of white on the Flatirons. Kiefer pedaled southbound up the hill (later to become known as "the Hill"), past the university, and quickly reached the open countryside, pulling his coat tight against the wind sweeping down from the foothills. Unlike demand for his bicycles, that wind never failed.

Soon he turned eastbound and put the wind at his back. The land around him was lumpy with golden hills and blowing grass. The area would become, during the next century, quite well-known among bicyclists and nuclear protesters, home to the Morgul-Bismark race course and Rocky Flats nuclear warhead trigger factory, respectively. Now it is substantially covered with rows of tan houses and cul-de-sacs.

Kiefer was flying along the dirt. He didn't go to Marshall, and he didn't go back to Boulder. His creditors were annoyed, but not terribly surprised.[14]

Hot Bikes

Implosions like Kiefer's signaled the end of the Bicycle Craze. Having observed a string of years with accelerating demand and banking on more of the same, the manufacturers over-manufactured and the dealers overbought. When sales flattened out in 1895, the industry was on the hook, and the smaller dealers were the first to buckle under the weight of their hopeful assumptions.

Eddie Kiefer's inglorious exit was notably low-key compared to that of many of his fellow economic refugees, whose weapon of choice, apparently, was a good arson. Several desperado shop owners decided to torch their own operations as the business unwound between 1895 and 1901, hoping to make insurance companies pay for their overstock if nobody else would. (It should be noted that Kiefer's shop survived a mysterious fire about one month before his southbound escape.[15] The merchandise was eventually auctioned. Strangely, there is no record of the shop being torched successfully.) Of course, lots of things were going up in flames in those days, including entire cities. In the bike shops and factories, accidental flare-ups and explosions were not uncommon due to clumsy use of liquid hydrocarbons, which were kept on hand for various legitimate, if ill-conceived, purposes. But the frequency of unexplained fires ticked upward steeply as sales declined.

In Long Branch, New Jersey, in July 1897, flames were discovered and snuffed out in Raymond's butter store, next to a struggling bicycle shop. "While looking for the origin of the fire the Fire Marshal discovered that several holes had been bored with an augur in the wooden partition between the two stores, and he claims that lighted paper and matches had been pushed through the holes."[16] Yeah, don't mess with the Fire Marshall.

Dozens of bicycle factories and parts factories were destroyed by suspicious fires in the late 1890s. Conflagrations engulfed the facilities of some of the biggest names in the business. Pope's six-story headquarters building in Boston went up, incinerating five thousand tires, almost two thousand bicycles, and Colonel Pope's Civil War memorabilia. On the loss of his relics, the Colonel commented: "I valued them more than anything else the fire destroyed."[17] A few months later a very similar inferno was visited upon another flagship of the industry, the Humber Bicycle Works in Coventry, England, with losses reported at £100,000. In December 1895, the Bergen Steel Mill's spoke-making operation and frame-tube building in New Jersey burned down after the night crew was mysteriously dismissed. Straight Manufacturing Company of Jamestown, New York; Wilhelm Bicycle Works, Hamburg, Pennsylvania; Budd Brothers, Saratoga; the Lobdell rim factory in Marietta, Ohio; Norwood Bicycle Works, Cincinnati; I. Silverman and Brothers, Chicago; Fowler Bicycle and Carriage Works, Chicago; Barnes Bicycle

Factory, Syracuse; Ellicott Cycle Manufacturing, Tonawanda, New York; the Brentwood tire factory on Long Island… The list goes on. All were destroyed in suspicious fires during the same period.[18] The bicycle industry went up in flames at the turn of the century.

Attempting to unload one's toxic financial obligations onto other parties has become a convention of American culture. You've got to feel for the SUV dealers, in an era of high-tech fire protection systems and masterful inspectors. Will the dealers get a spot at the bailout trough alongside the manufacturers? Keep an eye out for "eco-terrorists."

Camel Nation

We almost had camels. In 1853, faced with the increasing cost and general difficulty of hauling freight from the Kansas Territory to settlements in New Mexico, then Secretary of War Jefferson Davis introduced the idea of using camels for this task instead of inefficient oxen and mules. An initial test run with three dozen camels led Davis's successor to request the importation of one thousand more. Camels were on. But then the Civil War broke out, putting Project Dromedary on the back burner; and then the railroads finally crept their way over to the hinterlands of the Southwest, and the camel idea went by the wayside.[19] But hey, we almost had camels. We almost had cowboys sitting around the campfire, eating beans and riding the dusty trail with their trusty camels. Instead of

Trigger, Roy Rogers the Singing Cowboy could've had a camel named Spit. Camels were close. Not many people know this.

I bring up America's close call with camels to illustrate the point that seemingly intractable aspects of culture have been at the mercy of these little twists of fate, the larks and whims and prejudices of those in positions of power, the flashes of genius of inventors, and various other accidents of history. There is a lot of random chance involved. We could've had camels.

America also came close, in my opinion, to developing a full-fledged electric-car industry alongside or instead of the Church of Internal Combustion. With another invention or delay in an invention here and there, if there had been a Henry Ford for electric cars, things could have gone very differently. Electric and gasoline-powered vehicles were running neck and neck for a time. The Pope Company sold fleets of electric cabs in the 1890s; the system that was used for continuous remote recharging and replacing of spent batteries of the hansom cabs is not that different than the system proposed by Shai Agassi in 2008 for the entire country of Israel.

So we could have been a camel nation or an electric-car nation. Could this country have become a bicycle nation, like Holland or Denmark? That might be pushing it, but I like to think that it could have. If the motor revolution had been delayed a few years, or if the bursting of the bike bubble had occurred a little sooner, there might have been enough momentum from an industry on the ropes to push the widespread use of their product into the nation's farmlands and working-class neighborhoods. Cowboys and various other icons of American cool might have accepted and adopted it. Instead, they ignored it, or ridiculed and rejected the machine and its users, a stance which lives on today in the form of the occasional beer can hurled from a speeding pickup and the occasional Doppler-affected cry of "Git off the road idiot!" What we needed perhaps was a Henry Ford not only for electric cars but a Henry Ford for bicycles. Ford was selling brand-new Model T's in the 1920s for less than what people were paying for bicycles in the 1880s.

Of course, much of this turns on the price of gasoline. Had Americans not been sitting quite by accident on some of the world's most obscenely large oil reserves, the push and pull of history might have taken us down some wildly different roads on some wildly different vehicles. But we were, and it didn't, so here we are.

A Tool for Liberty and Oppression

Riding a wheel, our own powers are revealed to us…

Maria Ward, 1896[20]

Kim Jong Il, long-time dictator of North Korea, can't stand the sight of a woman on a bicycle. According to reports that have trickled out of the surreal regime, the Beloved Bespectacled Leader was so repulsed in 1996 by the vision of one random woman bicycling in pants that he declared bicycling off-limits for all women, and so it has been ever since. Many North Korean women rely on bicycles to such a degree that they have no choice but to continue using them, although they are said to jump off and walk whenever they see an agent of the government.

Kim Jong Il's attitude toward female bicyclists would not have seemed so off-the-wall in America during the 1890s. Largely because it provoked and exposed such backward thinking, bicycling advanced the cause of women's rights in many important ways in the nineteenth century. It was impossible to ride in the frilly Victorian get-ups of the time, so the women's rational "bicycling costume" appeared, pushing the boundaries of acceptable dress. As it came to be with driving years later, the mere act of learning to ride was liberating, as the trick of balance had been something that many thought too difficult or just unsuitable for a woman. After mastering the bicycle, she could then ride straight out of the city and go anywhere the roads went, free from antiquated social constraints and under her own power. She would sweat and feel the burn of hard exercise, most unladylike.

"Yearly they grow more confident in the management of their machines," noted the sporting monthly *Outing* in 1890. It was quite an understatement. The wheelmen would soon be moved to recalibrate their paternalistic attitudes toward female riders. In 1896, the top endurance bicyclist in the state of Colorado was identified only as Mrs. A. E. Rinehart. Mrs. Rinehart rode almost twenty thousand miles during the year, including one-hundred-twenty separate rides of at least one hundred miles, and set the state record for the two-hundred-mile distance.[21] She was apparently an awesome, and obsessive, rider, but just one of many women who would learn they were superior to most men in their power, endurance, and skills on the bike.

For many reasons the vision of a woman on a bicycle became a hot-button symbol for female power and freedom. Leaders in the movement were well aware of the bicycle's significance and talked it up, encouraging others to learn the wheel. Susan B. Anthony and Elizabeth Cady Stanton both praised the bicycle as idea in their speeches. Anthony said famously that the bicycle "had done more to emancipate women than anything else in the world" and that a female on a bike was "the picture of free, untrammeled womanhood"; Stanton said "women were riding to suffrage on the bicycle." These quote-lets are being discussed right now in a women's studies class somewhere.

Sadly, the association with the women's movement is about all bicyclists can claim in the realm of historic social advancement. Most of the social contributions of American bicyclists have been negative. The nineteenth-century League of American Wheelmen, for instance, was an aggressively class-conscious and racist organization. Although we should be cautious about equating the majority of the League's membership with the whole of bicyclists in America at that time, the League and the bicycling population at large seem to have been composed overwhelmingly of a certain type of rider: a wealthy, white city-dweller, riding for recreation. Bicycles were quite expensive items in the high-wheeler era and remained so through the early safety-bike years, generally out of reach for working-class people—there were no cheap department store–type bikes available like there are today—so the demographic fault line was set from the beginning.

When a wider swath of the unwashed masses began to acquire bicycles after the market was glutted in 1895, the proper wheelmen intensified their efforts to set themselves apart from these vulgar newcomers. As road rage incidents between bicyclists and pedestrians or teamsters became more frequent, and sentiment boiled up in crowded cities against the new silent swooper of the traffic grid, the Potters of the world popped up at every turn to disown the reckless hooligans. That's strikingly similar to what we've seen from the twenty-first-century equivalents of these factions. Back then they called themselves wheelmen; these days the word is "cyclists," and a diminishing percentage of riders receives their stamp of approval.* Even if bicycling becomes hugely popular in the United States, the "cyclists" will still comprise a small and exclusive faction, fighting in backhanded ways to preserve the original class symbolism of their expensive hobby.

---

*The proper wheelmen have always reserved their most pointed assaults for other bicyclists, and this is still true in a world dominated by cars. Of course, since different individuals have different ideas about just what "proper" means, the situation often arises where one self-described proper cyclist is going for the throat of another. This is grand entertainment, but not very productive. The atmosphere among "cycling advocates" these days is characterized by irreconcilable division over simple issues and repetitive vitriolic Internet postings. The level of acrimony in these exchanges is a bit shocking at times.

Circle of White Power

The historic snobbery of the wheelmen took some extreme forms. By February 1894 the issue of race had been central in the League's politics for some time. It was then that the new president of the LAW, Charles Luscomb, who rode into office on a sort of white-power platform, opened a meeting of the League's state delegates in Louisville, Kentucky. Luscomb introduced one W. W. Watts, who "took the floor to propose an amendment to the constitution drawing the color line by inserting the word 'white.' In a lengthy speech Mr. Watts assigned his reasons. He closed by declaring that if favorable action were taken upon the proposition an increase in membership of over 5,000 would follow from the South within a year. Mr. Watts was frequently applauded during his remarks." The measure passed with plenty of room to spare.[22]

The racist amendment to the LAW constitution remained in place for 105 years, not that it was noticed much. The forgotten amendment was finally repealed through the impetus of League president Earl Jones in 1999. The long life of the "whites only" clause can be forgiven to some extent as the League itself was a forgotten, useless shell for much of the amendment's existence. There was nobody minding the store, nobody around to read or care about the club's constitution, much less change it. (The League basically dropped off the radar from the Depression to the mid-1960s, when some bright-eyed folks sparked a reanimation.)

When he fixed the LAW constitution, Earl Jones also tried, symbolically, to fix another injustice, by granting the great racing champion Major Taylor membership in the League.[23] It is not certain that Taylor would have wanted this.

The Intolerance of the Wheelmen

The racism among bicyclists in the 1890s was, unfortunately, more that just a sign of the times. It was an extreme and pathetic manifestation of the same elitism and exclusivity that, for whatever reason, has haunted the bicycle from the very early days right on through the present. As this aggressive intolerance is still evident among today's wheelmen in varied forms, we may rightly wonder what the heck is going on there. It could simply be that there are self-righteous jerks sprinkled liberally throughout the entire human race, involved in all activities and every mode of transport, including bicycling. Or there may be something weird or special about bicycling that attracts these people. Sometimes it seems so. It could be that those with sniveling personalities—the instinctive joiners and excluders, the joiners-excluders—flock in disproportionate numbers to the bicycle. If bicycling is one of those things you do to set yourself apart from the rest of the world, then an increase in the popularity of bicycling runs counter to your agenda—a lot of people who come into the clubhouse seem to want to slam the door shut nastily behind them.

One thing is certain: We can't blame the pressure of automobiles for the acrimony that some bicyclists display toward the world around them, including other bicyclists, as the same sort of acrimony was in full effect before automobiles existed. Bicyclists were never out there singing "Kumbaya" with each other or their fellow road users—it's been conflict the whole way. It could simply be that the bicycle itself is a beacon of darkness, bitterness, and ill will that transforms anyone who climbs on top of it.

Since bicycles were invented, self-proclaimed masters of that domain have erected walls and placed arbitrary filters, riddles, clothing requirements, and icy glares—racial requirements—in front of anybody hoping to become a bicyclist. Clearly any effort to popularize the bicycle for basic transportation purposes will have to overcome some of the bicyclists themselves. A more annoying foe could hardly be imagined.

III

THE NEXT BIG THING

Faster than Fear

Mister Taylor, If you don't leave here before 48 hours you will be sorry. We mean business. Clear out if you value your life. [signed] White Riders

Text of a note left on Major Taylor's door in Savannah, Georgia, spring 1898, with skull and crossbones[1]

MARSHALL TAYLOR (LATER TO BE PROMOTED TO "MAJOR") was a young boy when his father started working as a teamster for the wealthy and white Southard family in Indianapolis. Marshall was also employed with the Southards, in a way, as a playmate for their son Daniel. Marshall and Dan became inseparable friends, eating, playing, and sitting down for private tutoring together in the Southard home. "The rest of Dan's playmates were of wealthy families too, and I was not in the neighborhood long before I learned to ride a bicycle just as they did," Taylor recalled. "All the boys owned bicycles, excepting myself, but Dan saw to it that I had one too." At that time there would have been almost zero chance, under normal circumstances, for a poor black kid to gain regular access to a bicycle. Thus Taylor, looking back on his amazing life from a world champion's perch, regarded his friendship with Dan Southard as the "freak of fate" that started it all.[2]

Young Marshall quickly learned that he was as smooth and fast on a bike as any kid in the neighborhood. But when Dan and the others walked into the gymnasium, Marshall wasn't allowed to follow. Conversely, Marshall spent so much of his time in the Southards' world that when he went home to visit his actual brothers and sisters they too regarded him as an outsider. He was caught in the middle from a very young age.

The racing career of Major Taylor started early, and so did the threats of violence from his white opponents. Nonwhites were then banned outright from racing on the track or even attending the races. As a teenager Taylor had to sneak his way into road races, securing special permission from race promoters, keeping his entry a secret, and delaying his arrival at the start until the very last second to minimize the inevitable commotion. In one early race on the roads around Indianapolis, he reached the finish far in the lead, driven mainly by fear of a physical attack his competitors had promised should he be caught. Taylor was inspired to serious competition by "Birdie" Munger and the friendly legend Arthur Zimmerman, who recognized the championship potential and became father figures to Taylor, but these helpful bicyclists were outnumbered by the bulk of racers, some of whom emanated sustained loathing at Taylor as man and symbol. As his career progressed, Taylor continued to find himself banned from many venues and important races and otherwise faced constant hurdles, for instance, in securing the same food and lodging that the other racers enjoyed.

But young Taylor's speed was impossible to ignore. He was beating the top racers and, increasingly, race fans demanded to see him. So plenty of promoters welcomed him warmly, with dollar signs in their eyes. One-on-one matchups between Taylor and other famous racers of the day were often marketed as epic battles of Black versus White. Come see what "the colored boy" can do against McDuffee, Cooper, or the Butler brothers. There was a long line of challengers, but only one "Dusky Champion."

On the track Taylor was subjected to more than his fair share of the rough treatment that was considered a normal part of the sport. Other racers would often team up illicitly and try to block him or wreck him. One newspaper noted: "There is a lot of cheap sporting blood in certain of the cycle racers, and it never has showed more clearly than in the case of Taylor, who, as a rider, is really superior to most of them."[3] But Taylor, though by no means unbeatable, was just too fast and too damn good, most days. And he looked good while he crushed his opponents. Taylor took pride in being the smoothest as well as the fastest. His pedaling technique produced efficient speed, while conserving energy; it was also, said Taylor, "an easy, graceful celerity of motion that was pleasing to the eye."[4] All of it—the smooth skills, the winning of races that had been fixed against him, the calm demeanor, the black skin—it was just too much for some.

On September 23, 1897, things came to a head in Taunton, Massachusetts. Racers were soft-pedaling after crossing the line in the mile open final when W. E. Becker jumped from his bike onto Taylor's back. The men crashed onto the track, where Becker choked Taylor into unconsciousness. Taylor was out for fifteen minutes. Becker was disqualified and fled from an angry crowd of fans. He fouled me, Becker explained.[5]

Becker's choking of Taylor ignited less talk about Becker's outrageous attack than about what should be done with Taylor. Not long after the incident the regular "Gossip of the Cyclers" column in the *New York Times* intoned: ". . . many argue that restricting the negro to races with his kind or to team races against white teams will put him on a better standing with the other riders and the general public."[6] Many would have felt more comfortable if Taylor would have raced against himself in some kind of one-man Negro Racing League. Before long some of the most prominent racers were working to have him banned from racing altogether.

Major Taylor versus Tom Cooper

European stage races, and in particular the spectacle of the Tour de France, have defined the sport of bicycle racing for the past fifty years in the eyes of the world. In the 1890s, in sharp contrast, the most intense and prestigious cycle races took place in the United States, on steeply banked oval tracks with ice-smooth wood surfaces. Most of the track races were short, geared toward raw speed and action rather than endurance. Races like the one-mile or five-mile were the premier events of the program, with the action usually exploding in the final lap.* Crowds of the 1890s loved a good speed record. In many of the events, the racers drafted behind strong colleagues on bikes built to carry two, three, four, sometimes five riders to keep the speed high. The American Cycle Racing Association (ACRA), Major Taylor's sponsor, kept forty to fifty eager pacers on salary at the Manhattan Beach track.

The speed of the races, the intensity of the competition, even the machines (at least the singles) were very similar to what is seen in bicycle track racing today. The velodrome is lost in time. Those who have ever watched bicycle track racing—say a match sprint or points race—are well on their way to imagining what the racing was like in Major Taylor's era. This is especially true of Japanese keirin racing, with its "dernies"—small motorcycles designed specifically for pacing cyclists on velodrome tracks. Unfortunately, very few Americans out there have ever seen any track racing other than NASCAR. Bike racing, of course, was the NASCAR of the 1890s.

Tom Cooper, a clean-cut and unusually tall bike racer from Detroit, was as well known as Dale Junior in his day. In 1896 Cooper sprinted to a national championship (there

---

*The public developed a taste for much longer races on the track as well as the road. Major Taylor was one of many top racers who dabbled in longer races, even giving six-day racing a shot. During his first six-day race he rode eighteen hours in a single uninterrupted stretch, but sprints remained his bread and butter.

was often some ambiguity about championships in this era due to competing racing organizations) and continued to mix it up at the very top for three years. He traveled to France in 1900 and showed quite well. He was moderately famous and plenty rich. By the time he faced Major Taylor in the summer of 1901, for a long-awaited matchup between two established champs, Cooper was looking toward a career beyond racing.

Major Taylor had been itching for a race with Cooper for many years, and not just because Cooper was one of the top sprinters in the world. Major Taylor considered Cooper to be one of the two riders, along with Eddy "Cannon" Bald, who had put the most energy into his persecution over the years. As an officer in the racers' union, Cooper was at the front of an effort to get Taylor banned from racing for life, and Taylor knew it.* He had faced Bald and Cooper in final heats a number of times, on the track with a number of other riders, but he yearned to take them out behind the woodshed and punish each of them one-on-one. Bald, who had captured the national championship three years in a row, flat-out refused to face Taylor in a match sprint; the "Cannon's" personal code prohibited his racing head-to-head against any dark-skinned opponent. So Taylor turned his attention to Cooper, who hemmed and hawed and avoided the challenge for several years. They finally met for a race when Cooper got back from

---

*Wrote Taylor in his autobiography: "Cooper was treasurer of the American Cyclists' Racing Union at the time and he was one of the principal instigators who aimed to debar me for life from bicycle racing tracks of the world."[7] Taylor also singled out Floyd MacFarland as being particularly hateful. Cooper, Bald, and MacFarland were three of the very best racers in the world and also very influential in the sport.

France in 1900, but Cooper declared the track unfit at the last minute and the race was canceled. The next year Cooper saw he could avoid the duel no longer. It didn't look good for him when he requested prior to the race that the losing rider should receive some prize money as well, instead of the originally agreed-upon winner-take-all. Taylor refused.

As the riders went through their pre-race rituals, Cooper's trainer, Tom Eck, started trash talking, as was his custom. Taylor recalled Eck telling his own manager: "Well, Bawb, Tawm will now proceed to hand your little darkey the most artistic trimming of his young life." Eck's mouth was writing checks that Cooper's legs couldn't cash. Taylor crushed Cooper and his 108-inch gear* unambiguously, taking the first two heats of the best-of-three match. Crossing the line far ahead of his rival, Taylor did something that he had never done before in his career: He added unnecessary distance to his margin of victory, just to make Cooper look bad. "If ever a race was run for blood this one was," he explained.[8]

Next Big Thing

Major Taylor's drubbing of Tom Cooper vaulted him further into international stardom. Cooper had done very well on his recent European tour and now Taylor had crushed Cooper

---

*Bicycle gearing is expressed in distance traveled per pedal revolution. Cooper's 108-inch gear was large even for racing. Taylor noticed during the race that Cooper was using an unusually large gear and he used tactics to neutralize it.

like a bug; the Euros beckoned the Major to ship himself over. He did so the following season, and trimmed the bigheaded French champ Edmund Jacquelin to much acclaim. But Major Taylor was in fact not the Next Big Thing.

As for Cooper, the lopsided loss to the man he'd unsuccessfully tried to ban wasn't exactly the blaze of glory he'd been looking for. He continued racing through the summer, with mixed results. A week after losing to Taylor, he met him again at Madison Square Garden, but the two raced in different events. Taylor won his. Cooper blew a tire at the start of his preliminary heat; he won his second-chance heat but finished out of the money in the final, highly uncharacteristic.[9] In late August at a race in Washington, Cooper failed to qualify for the final for the first time since he turned pro. He won the consolation race, which was small consolation. It sounds like this particular final may have been a good one to miss, however, as it ended with Floyd MacFarland crashing, then punching Iver Lawson in the face.*[10] A few days later

---

*Floyd MacFarland was a fiery individual with a tendency to start fights. In his history of American bicycle racing, Peter Nye writes: "While at a champagne reception in Camperdown, in Victoria, Australia, MacFarland was reputed to have deliberately insulted Bull Williams, a professional boxer. The two men squared off and MacFarland knocked his opponent flat."[11] After retiring from racing, MacFarland became a very successful race promoter and manager, trading in his bike shorts for a three-piece suit and a bowler hat. At the Newark velodrome in April 1915, MacFarland got into it with a concessionaire named David Lantenberg who wanted to hang some banners around the track. As the encounter escalated from yelling match to physical scuffle, the much smaller Lantenberg, who was holding a screwdriver, swung at MacFarland and stabbed him behind the ear with the tool, killing him. Lantenberg maintained the blow was inadvertent and was later acquitted of manslaughter.[12] Major Taylor said that MacFarland exuded "hatred" for him both on and off the track.

Cooper salvaged his pre-retirement run when he won a final heat at the Hartford velodrome after avoiding a three-rider crash; one of the crashed riders was Iver Lawson, who veered off the track and launched into the crowd, injuring some spectators.[13] It was a rough summer for many racers besides Cooper. Major Taylor himself had bad luck after the match with Cooper, missing many of the August races after a hard fall on the track in Boston. It was a summer of blood and bitterness for the top professionals.

On October 10, 1901, we find Tom Cooper back in his hometown of Detroit, hanging out at the Grosse Pointe horse-racing track. There weren't any horses running at Grosse Pointe that day. Instead, a strange new breed was gathered there: motorheads. Among them was Henry Ford. In fact, Ford turned out to be the star of the day, winning one of the earlier automobile races on record. Ford drove his latest offering rather slowly and unspectacularly around the dirt oval, beating exactly one opponent, Alexander Winton, after Winton's car sputtered and died.* It wasn't much of a race, but Winton was known as the man to beat among racing pioneers, and in besting him Ford gained a critical mass of recognition and respect as an auto builder. It was perhaps the most significant event in his professional life.

---

*Like so many others Alexander Winton had come to auto racing by way of bicycle manufacturing. Winton's engine manufacturing division was purchased by General Motors in 1930, and, as General Motors' Electro-Motive Division, the factory built the huge engines for the streamlined diesel locomotives that killed steam power in the United States. Electro-Motive continued building locomotive engines (and submarine engines for the U.S. Navy) through the twentieth century.

The fastest thing on the track that day, most likely, was the motor-assisted tandem bicycle exhibited by Tom Cooper and his buddy Barney Oldfield. When the impending doom of obsolescence cast its shadow over their sport prior to the turn of the century, bicycle race promoters started importing French-made motorized pace bicycles, which pioneered the development of motorcycles. But the crowd at Grosse Pointe wasn't interested in bicycles, motorized or otherwise. The novelty of motorbikes and motor pacing was already wearing thin by 1901. They yawned in the general direction of the two bike racers and their motor tandem.[14]

The winds of change were in the air, and they smelled like burning rubber.

999

Just prior to Ford's historic victory, Tom Cooper was seen taking a lap around the track with Henry Ford and, according to a Detroit newspaper, giving him some advice on how to approach the competition.[15] Perhaps it was then that Cooper became hooked.

Cooper left Detroit that winter to run a coal mine in southwestern Colorado, something closely resembling work. On March 16 the following spring, the *Detroit Free Press* proclaimed: "Tom Cooper is back from the mines."[16] Cooper was through with mining for good. He had already been in contact with Henry Ford, perhaps as far back as the Grosse

Pointe race, eagerly imploring him, "Let's make a race car. My money and your expertise." Ford was not inclined to turn down a large infusion of cash and the chance to break free of his financial backers. Although Ford's wife, Clara, didn't trust Cooper, noting his association with "low down women," Ford accepted his offer and set out to make the most beastly race car yet created.*[17]

A small group worked on the 999, named after a famously fast locomotive, in the back of Barton Peck's Detroit bicycle shop. When it was rolled out in late summer 1902, it caused a minor sensation in the press and maybe even a few shudders of fear in the men who created it. With its crude frame and exposed engine it looked like a monstrous industrial go-cart. The driver sat up high behind the engine, completely unprotected, gripping a crude T-bar that served as a steering wheel. The engine itself was the largest gas engine that had ever been attached to a vehicle. The builders figured the car might do over one hundred miles per hour, which they estimated from road tests during which an ever present mechanic named Ed "Spider" Huff crawled all over the machine making adjustments and leaning this way and that to act as ballast.**

At some point Cooper and Ford had a falling out. It's unclear exactly what happened. Clara Ford wrote that Henry

---

*After Ford broke ties with them to go into business with Cooper, his former backers formed the Cadillac auto company. Mrs. Ford's feelings are made fairly clear in her letters.[18]

**Ford and his associates, most notably Spider Huff and Harold Wills, actually built two similar race cars that summer, the 999 and one they called the Arrow.

"caught him in a number of sneaky tricks."[19] It's possible that Cooper had somehow sabotaged the car's performance to gain full possession of it under more favorable terms. In any case Ford felt cheated and came around to an opinion of Tom Cooper similar to that held by his wife and Major Taylor, and the race car ended up in Cooper's hands.

Cooper recruited the toughest and craziest bastard he knew to drive the untamed 999, Barney Oldfield. Climbing aboard the 999, Oldfield went from a strong but obscure amateur bicycle racer to perhaps the most famous figure in American sports. With Oldfield in the driver's seat, drifting the devil's go-cart through the dirt turns at over sixty miles per hour, the Ford-Cooper 999 blew the doors off every other car in existence—at least, it would have, if those other cars had doors. It's a good thing they didn't, or they would have lost them. For the first time auto racing—motoring in general—displayed the kind of speed and smooth violence that would make it a compelling spectacle for the next hundred-plus years. Even though Ford had broken acrimoniously from Cooper, people still knew him as the builder of the frightening-looking car that Oldfield was using to tear up tracks around the country, and he leveraged that association to start the Ford Motor Company.

The 999 was an unholy love child. Its riotous success was the freakish product of Ford's ingenuity, Cooper's winnings, and Oldfield's guts. Now, every time I sit down to watch NASCAR on Sunday, cooler of beer next to the couch, and spare cooler behind the couch, I know I'm watching something that has its roots in bicycle track racing. Some NASCAR fans get a little agitated, in Southern accents, when I point out that it was pedal-pushers who pioneered auto racing. Sorry, NASCAR fans. That's the way history operates. You've got to look back beyond Daytona Beach to see how this whole thing started. Mark Martin may as well be wearing bike shorts under his fire suit.

The Death of Tom Cooper

When the auto age came along, Tom Cooper dropped his bike and grabbed on. Soon the ex-champ was known as a promoter of car races and a driver—"chauffeur" was then an accepted term for a race car driver, betraying the early auto's strong French heritage. Cooper and Oldfield were just two of many bicycle racers who crossed over to racing cars, or attempted to. These guys found very quickly that, without the safety belts and metal cages that protect modern drivers, driving fast in one of these homemade jalopies around several other equally inexperienced drivers in their jalopies was about the most perilous thing a person could do, somewhere between bike racing and standing up in front of a hail of bullets from a Maxim gun. To some of them, no doubt, the danger was part of the attraction. The early cars took all the danger of bike racing and strapped a motor to it. The physics were unkind. Eventually some of Oldfield's beautiful sliding turns devolved into zigzagging detours through the fences and into the crowd—mental note: put up some barriers there.* The bloodiness of the racing did nothing to diminish its growing popularity.

In 1906 Tom Cooper was traveling the country racing cars and promoting six-day bicycle races. Automobiles had advanced a great deal in the five years since the premier of the 999. His latest rig was a big Matheson, much more refined than the Ford-Cooper and faster to boot.** In late November Cooper was in New York City and cruising around Central Park with several friends packed into the Matheson roadster. Just before midnight Cooper got caught up in a race with another driver. Cooper got the better of his anonymous rival, for a moment, but the seasoned veteran on the racetrack was about to fall victim to the chaos of city traffic. Just as the impromptu race was revving up, another car was running out of gas on the West Drive near the Seventy-seventh Street entrance. Its chauffeur pulled the stalled car to the side and went to fetch some gas while the car's owner waited in the back seat. The stalled car was lying in wait when Cooper's Matheson came speeding over the rise at fifty miles per hour. The Matheson clipped the car, swerved harshly, and rolled. "In

---

*In a magazine interview Barney Oldfield noted: "I got so I didn't call going through the fence an accident unless I got hurt going through or hurt someone else on the other side."[20] Oldfield's crashes killed three spectators and injured several others in his first two years as a driver. His first major accident occurred after he had quit the 999 and was driving Alexander Winton's Baby Bullet. Earl Kiser, the star bicyclist known as the "Match Race King," crippled himself in a crash during a race against Oldfield in 1905.

**Colonel Pope's son Harold Linden Pope, who had worked as a draftsman for his father's bicycle company, would soon gain acclaim as the designer of Matheson's highly successful "Silent Six" engine, which was produced from 1909 to 1912.[21]

its aerial revolution it pitched Cooper and everybody in the car high into the air." Tom Cooper was dead at the scene, with two others mortally wounded. Cooper's female companion, an actress named Virginia Levick, was the only survivor.[22]

The Death of Major Taylor

Even Major Taylor turned into a motorhead. In the spring of 1905, Taylor was stopped twice for speeding on the main street of his hometown of Worcester and fined $35 for street racing. In contrast to Tom Cooper's Pennsylvania-built Matheson, Taylor's car was French.

After the final capitulation of the bike-racing phase of his life, Taylor sought like so many others to break into the auto business. He came up with a unique idea, perhaps much too unique, for a sprung steel "tire" that he hoped would address the problem of poor tire durability that car owners were then experiencing. Taylor's old mentor Birdie Munger had marketed his own successful auto part and tried to help Taylor launch his. Whether it was the vision of a genius or the ridiculous notion of a hack, the Metal Taylor Tire never hit the market.

Considering not only his racing palmarès but all the unbelievable crap he had to deal with, it's no stretch to call Major Taylor the best bike racer of his day. He clawed through racist barriers just to participate in his sport—fifty years before Jackie Robinson's entry into pro baseball—and then came out on top even though the other racers teamed up to make his life miserable. But his story does not end well.

When his speed deserted him, Taylor didn't have much to fall back on. The entire sport was fading. There were no lucrative endorsement deals, media jobs, or coaching opportunities for retired champions in those days. He was denied admission to the local engineering school. When his automotive invention and the Taylor Manufacturing Company failed, he began to slip down the ladder. Records show that he worked as a machinist and then as an auto mechanic. In 1925 he sold the upscale home that he had owned for twenty-five years and moved into an apartment with his increasingly distraught wife. In 1929 he self-published his autobiography and then drove from town to town trying to sell it.

Taylor's health had been declining precipitously along with his finances. A bad case of shingles required increasingly frequent and lengthy hospitalizations. In 1932 he went to Chicago to sell his book and wound up in the hospital. Completely broke by this point, he was transferred to the county charity ward, where he died of heart failure at fifty-three. The world had forgotten bicycle racing and had forgotten Major Taylor. The former champion of the world was buried in an unmarked grave.[23]

IV

USES

The Utility Bicycle

EVEN THOUGH IT WAS BEING USED PRIMARILY AS SPORTING equipment, the bicycle gave late-nineteenth-century Americans the strong impression of a machine that would be useful for a wide range of highly important, no-nonsense purposes. The simple and unsexy act of riding to work was rarely mentioned, perhaps because urban rail systems were ubiquitous and did the job well enough. Much more excitement was generated about the bicycle's prospects for use in more serious and manly pursuits like policing, putting out fires, and killing people—"The Official Vehicle of Very Official Things" is how a recent magazine ad for Range Rover put it.

Cops on bikes made the long arm of the law a little longer. New York City bike cops mounted for duty to match two-wheeled scorchers, who had generated a pile of complaints, but chased down runaway horses and scofflaw cart drivers on their first day. (Ten years later the city employed more than one hundred bike cops.) In an even more obvious application, bicycle couriers began to deliver a wide variety of goods, parcels, and messages—the mundane wheels of commerce. The city of Chicago went with full-on bicycle delivery of the mail after testing bikes against mounted and foot-bound postmen. In 1894 the Cincinnati office of Bell Telegraph put thirty of their inspectors on bikes.[1]

The same year rumors drifted across the country that Parisians were tooling around on motorized bicycles—even as the bicycle was coming up to speed, the rumble of motors could be heard in the American press. The pedal-cycle was tossed into a sort of existential crisis at the height of its momentum. By 1897 it was clear that the horseless-carriage dream would be realized. Electric and gasoline-powered carriages were being exhibited left and right. When four New York businessmen came up with an idea that year to produce a cargo bike called the "Klondike Bicycle," designed to haul five-hundred-pound loads of mining equipment to the Alaskan goldfields, their idea came a few years too late and perhaps on the wrong side of the world.[2]

Impenetrable Advance Cloud

The bicycle's potential for use in war, the most official use of all, generated a great deal of speculation and haughty pronouncements. Sergeant Hugh J. Barron, a booster for the militarization of the bicycle and enthusiastic member of an organization called the United States Military Wheelmen, explained how he thought, or hoped, bikes could be used in battle: "The cyclist, in the early stage of operations, will act as an impenetrable advance cloud or screen for the army, pushing far ahead into the enemy's theatre of operations, making his power felt long before the armies have a chance to come together, paralyzing the enemy's communications." Perhaps at that point dazzling them with bike tricks. If that doesn't work, the bicycle corps may "act as the anvil for the main army to hammer the enemy against."[3] That's a lot more intense than riding to the office.

Is there possibly a hint of desperation in the sergeant's projection? It could be that some wheelmen experienced crises of masculinity when their hobby, which had always been associated with a certain level of male sexual indignity in rural and working-class sectors of society, was adopted by large numbers of young women and became a symbol of female empowerment. One big, dusty, glorious bicycle battle could take care of that. They'll never laugh at the wheelmen again after they hear of our exploits in battle, wheeling back and forth over the corpses of our enemies, just for fun.

Anyone could see there were fatal flaws in the fantasy of bicycling into large set-piece battles. "It is a very simple matter to ride on horseback over a plowed field," explained a critic of this vision in 1894, "but to ride over the same field on a bicycle would be an impossibility. If the enemy would consent to fight only on smooth roads, he could, of course, be charged with terrible effect by a regiment of cyclists." Ouch. Killjoy. Furthermore, "even if the battlefield should happen to be smooth the enemy need only fire a few loads of carpet tacks to render the ground quite impassable to bicycles with pneumatic tires."[4] So the combat bicyclist would need some kind of suitable surface. On the other hand, a bicycle wouldn't get shot, spooked, or hungry, or speak unexpectedly when nobody else was around. But neither the boosters nor the critics had anticipated the surreal and horrible turn warfare would take in coming years.

Boosters like Sergeant Barron may have had the backing of or may simply have been shills for bike makers like Pope, who were eager to see their products rolled into the military-industrial complex. In 1892 Colonel Pope, a Civil War vet, published two military drill manuals for bicyclists, by two different authors. In 1896 his company sent a special wheel to the annual exposition at Madison Square Garden. It had a forty-pound Colt machine gun attached to the top tube.[5] Applications for today's traffic come to mind, sure. Ironically, Pope's aggressive creation was a sign that the end was near for the entire military bike-versus-horse debate—because the arrival of the machine gun developed by Hiram Maxim's father, among other developments in industrialized killing, signaled a quick end to the concept of the cavalry charge.

Many decades later in the jungles of Southeast Asia, bicycles would prove very effective for waging war, although not in the way Sergeant Barron expected.

Flying Pigeons

People tend to believe that the dominant mode of transportation in a nation says profound things about the fundamental makeup of that nation and the people in it, that it's somehow predetermined by ingrained nature and established cultural traditions—the genes of the nation. Transportation is imagined to be a window into the national soul. In this narrative Americans drive cars and burn so much energy because of some peculiar American-ness; the Dutch ride bikes due to their quirky yet cute Euro tendencies, which allow them to embrace things like utility cycling and semi-legalized psychotropic drugs. But old-fashioned chance and the sometimes illogical decisions of individual humans seem to be as important as cultural or geographical predetermination in bringing different modes to dominance. The accidents of history are what created the "national character" in the first place. Dwelling on the substantially arbitrary course of history can bring on fits of what Milan Kundera called "the unbearable lightness of being."

We might someday see, here in this country, a swift and dramatic change in direction in transport paradigms that were assumed to be culturally ingrained and unalterable, like flipping a switch. It wouldn't be the first time.

The history of the bicycle in China provides an interesting example of how these things may or may not work. Many who think of transportation in China immediately envision a river of bicyclists flowing through a giant hazy city among throngs of pedestrians, motorbikes, and rickshaws. Although things have begun to change rapidly away from this vision in the past decade, with unimaginable numbers of Chinese dumping their bikes and getting into new cars, that familiar vision of China as a bicycling nation has been generally accurate for half a century. What is it about China, or the Chinese character, that made this possible? Nothing in particular, could very well be the answer.

Bicycles came to China in the 1890s in the hands of a relative few progressive Chinese who had been abroad to Europe or the United States. Like much of what came back to China in those days, bicycles were not just novel technology but symbolic of a radically different culture, of modernity itself. When Chinese rode them conspicuously around their towns for all to see, bicycles represented an eagerness to break free of stifling traditions and move on, literally and figuratively. Bicycling was a deliberately provocative act. Here again is the bicycle as idea, aggressively deployed against an array of oppressive traditions, as it had been in the women's movement abroad. So bicycling sprouted in China not as an outgrowth of the traditional culture, in which the preferred method of travel was to be hauled upon a litter like some kind of tribal chief, but as a slap against it. Bicycling was extremely un-Chinese.[6]

As it had been at one time in the United States, bicycling in China around the turn of the century was the domain of a privileged few, and the machines were expensive, scarce, and built for sport—imported—not the clunky black commie utility bikes we see in our Far East visions. The Chinese were perhaps less fired up about utility cycling than were Americans. This paradigm persisted for several decades. Then domestic production began in the mid-1930s, and prices plummeted. In 1941 occupied Shanghai was patrolled by Japanese on bikes and infiltrated by bicyclists smuggling rice, illuminating the possibilities of bicycling for serious purposes. But the revolutionary Communist regime is really what turned China into Bicycle Nation in 1949, with sweeping government edicts subsidizing manufacture, purchase, and use of bicycles. Before long there were rivers of bicyclists on black bicycles in China. Like flipping a switch.

The Chinese Communist leadership, looking for a way to get their population moving in an efficient fashion, chose the bicycle. The United States, swimming in wealth and oil, threw its weight behind the automobile.

Official Things

Even the long-legged Englishmen could not escape our troops on bicycles.

> Colonel Masanobu Tsuji, *Singapore: The Japanese Version,* 1961 (later published as *Japan's Greatest Victory, Britain's Worst Defeat,* 1997)[7]

While progressive Chinese were jabbing their elders with the idea of the bicycle, other Asian countries were well on the way to widespread adoption of the machine for mundane utilitarian purposes. Largely this was due to the surging Japanese bicycle industry, which had exported a staggering number of cheap, well-built bicycles to neighboring countries in the decades prior to World War II.

After Colonel Masanobu Tsuji scouted Malaya in 1941 to plan the Japanese invasion of the peninsula, he decided he would put his troops on bicycles for the long attack south to Singapore. Tsuji later wrote that two divisions had been outfitted with six thousand bicycles each prior to the invasion, but many other sources say that the Japanese simply commandeered their bicycles from Malays upon arrival. There were plenty to go around.

Troops landed on Malaya about eighty minutes after the Zeros swept into Pearl Harbor. Accompanied by tanks and trucks filled with their big guns and heavy equipment, Tsuji's invaders extracted full advantage from Japan-built bicycles and the Brits' paved plantation roads, rolling about six hundred miles to Singapore. This was no ordinary charity ride. The bicycle troops stabbed into enemy territory, using secondary tracks to encircle allied forces mired in their armored columns on the main road—stuck in a traffic jam, essentially, where the armor was a fat target for airplanes and big guns. Motors in flames, the British soldiers were forced to hoof it, and were quickly overtaken by troops on two-wheelers. When the allies blew the bridges, the Japanese waded across with their bikes and kept rolling. "With the infantry on bicycles," Tsuji explained, "there was no traffic congestion or delay." Tsuji claimed that a conventional campaign without bicycles would have taken over a year. The British defenses were wiped out in seventy days.[8]

Allied soldiers who were hiding along the route watched orderly columns of hundreds of Japanese soldiers pedaling by and happily talking among themselves as if headed to a picnic.[9]

These guys were in high spirits, at least at first. With extremely long days on the road, hauling sixty to eighty pounds of gear under their seats, pausing frequently for combat and chasing Englishmen into the jungle on foot, the rolling infantry started to feel the burn. Upon arrival at Singapore they were a hungry, saddle-weary bunch, but captured what was supposedly an impregnable fortress easily enough despite their saddle sores.

The British seemed shocked. They hadn't expected to be blitzkrieged by bicyclists. Decades later they still seemed shocked, and embarrassed. It was a particularly humiliating way to get skunked—to have this old British invention, viewed as a child's toy by many Englishmen in 1941, turned against them in such devastating fashion. Even without the bicycles the loss of Singapore would have been the most humiliating military defeat the British had ever suffered. That the Japanese had achieved this victory via bicycle was beyond the pale. Most British histories of the campaign preferred not to mention Tsuji's two-wheeled stratagem at all. Instead they dwelled on the Japanese use of tanks.[10] Some big, bad tanks those were. Grrrr.

The British forces in Malaya had plenty of tanks themselves. According to Tsuji, the Allies enjoyed a two-to-one superiority in tanks and armored vehicles, big guns, and infantrymen.[11] In the end the bicycles mattered more. The British defenders brought knives to a gunfight, as the saying goes, in more ways than one. Tsuji was unambiguous and unflowery about his bicycle advantage: "This was the reason why they were continually driven off the road into the jungle, where, with their retreat cut off, they were forced to surrender."

Adoption of Colonel Tsuji as an ideological bike brother has been hampered by numerous factors, particularly his hateful, fanatical disposition and involvement in multiple episodes of murder of prisoners of war in Malaya, the Philippines, and Burma. The story of his eating the liver of a captured American pilot one evening during the Burma campaign doesn't help much either.

Unofficial Things

There is little in history like Tsuji's campaign on Malaya, with columns of troops advancing on bicycles as planned. These were scenes at least somewhat reminiscent of Sergeant Barron's bike-cavalry fantasies. I imagine the sergeant's bones vibrating a bit in an ornate coffin as the invasion unfolds.

Nobody expected to be blitzkrieged in deliberate fashion by bicycle troops, but the bike did play a role in the battle for Europe. British paratroopers held folding bicycles as they floated down into Arnhem, a bridge too far. Photographs show Canadian troops on D-Day hauling bikes off the transports onto the beaches of Normandy. It was more common to find bicycles utilized spontaneously in the chaotic meltdown stages of warfare, as when German soldiers commandeered them from French villagers to scramble away from the rout on the western front.

Bicycles found many uses on the fringes and back sides of military operations. In many wars bikes had been used extensively and effectively for delivering messages and scouting; various occupying armies thus viewed use of the bicycle as something to be strictly controlled or even banned, if possible. Riding at night, especially, was regarded as highly suspicious behavior under many regimes, and rightly so. Some effective saboteurs and scouts did their best work at night, moving silently on bicycles through the French countryside or jungles of Asia.

There is a well-known photograph of Parisians streaming toward the Arc de Triomphe on their bikes to celebrate their liberation at the end of World War II. On the back of each vehicle is a large license plate with meticulously painted numbers—a requirement of the Nazi overlords. Decades earlier the British had attempted to strictly regulate the use of bicycles by the Boers. The occupiers weren't worried about traffic safety.[12]

Protest

Critical Mass is . . . what the hell is it anyway? To be honest, I'm not exactly sure what Critical Mass is, and nobody else is either. The nebulousness of the event is part of the draw. Those who take part in these infamous group rides, staged once a month in cities throughout North America, give multiple reasons for their involvement. Many are there for the social scene. Lots of young people rolling around in tight pants. Others get involved as activists. To them Critical Mass is a rolling protest against car culture. The official non-official Web site of the movement says, "Critical Mass's aim is to make people take notice of cyclists as road users." Some Massers have been more aggressive than others in their effort to transmit this message, and there have been some flare-ups here and there during the rallies with recalcitrant motorists. Let's face it, some are there for the flare-ups.

Critical Mass may indeed be misguided as advocacy or even as protest—if you said it was counterproductive, I'd be hard-pressed to disagree. As someone who recognizes and relishes the superior freedom that bicycling provides, I can't help but feel the earnest Massers are barking up the wrong tree. Perhaps their premise is flawed on a fundamental level. But Critical Mass is hardly the end of the world. It's not the threat to public welfare that it's perceived to be by officials in several cities.

I've been in exactly one Critical Mass. My presence there was a complete accident. Trying to get home from downtown one evening during the week of the Democratic National Convention, when the streets were completely sectioned off by riot cops and squelched into submission with roadblocks and traffic jams everywhere, I thought I had finally escaped from the mess when I ran into the back of the Mass—and its comically large entourage of cops on motos and bicycles, in squad cars, following with the famous riot SUVs and empty vans for potential arrestees. I think they even had a Bear in the Air. I've seen Dick Cheney's motorcade, and it didn't involve nearly as many armed security personnel as this.

For a quarter mile or so I had little choice but to roll along with the group. I would have loved to blast right through and head home, but I'd heard enough eyewitness accounts of past Critical Mass rides in Denver and other American cities to know that any false move could very well lead to my being gang-tackled by cops and having my bike disappeared to the impound lot. Who knows what kind of molestations might ensue. I saw a friend at the back of the group who was in the same predicament—how many others were in the group by default? There was a good-natured atmosphere among the Massers. Even the police, some of whom were on brand-new red Kawasaki dirt bikes, seemed to be enjoying themselves. Not much traffic was being blocked, other than myself. Some people walking on the sidewalk smiled and even cheered as the group rolled by, about one hundred strong. Then I turned off at first opportunity and went home, but only because I was dead tired and needed to get some dinner. The ride itself was plenty inviting. While these things have been known to devolve into orgies of self-loathing, I doubt any pepper spray got launched that evening.

Considering the substantially benign nature of the disruption caused by Critical Mass, the reaction of the New York City police to these rallies has been absolutely bizarre in its intensity. Granted, the Critical Mass rides in Manhattan were drawing huge numbers of riders compared to other cities—thousands—but the enthusiasm displayed by the police in their attempts to surveil, control, and quash the rides led many to suggest that they must be practicing for something else. Tension came to a head at a particularly large CM before the Republican National Convention in 2004. More than two hundred fifty riders were herded into a pen and arrested, most for parading without a permit. The city is still dealing with the flurry of lawsuits that followed the mass arrest, and the city's weird war with Critical Mass continues.[13]

It's common to find relative newcomers to bicycling banding together into these herds—Critical Mass rallies, organized tours, and club rides. It's a natural and to some degree useful tendency, providing psychological assurance and facilitating the flow of folk knowledge to new riders. The bicyclist will not scale freedom's heights in a herd, however. Freedom belongs to the solitary mountain cat, not the skittish herd of deer. Be a mountain cat.

The Bicycle Bomber

Our bikes have been used for many purposes. You can never control who has them.

> Sherwood Ross, former owner of Ross Bicycle
> Company, after a Ross bicycle was found in
> the trash near an Army recruitment station
> that had been bombed in 2008[14]

In a strange, maybe profound twist—or a simple continuation of a long line through history—the various American security apparatuses of this century, from Homeland Security on down to Wackenhut, have fixed their suspicious gaze on the bicycle, viewing it as something that poses an extraordinary challenge to law and order in these interesting times. Perhaps the Critical Mass rallies and associated incidents have spurred this mindset along, but there is no rational accounting to be made of the reflexive treatment of bicycling as suspicious, borderline criminal activity.*

The New York police were already in overkill mode going into '08. It didn't help bike PR in New York when, earlier in the year, security cameras caught a bicyclist apparently placing a makeshift bomb that blasted out the window and door of the Army recruiting station in Times Square at four in the morning. The incident was similar to early-morning attacks against the Mexican and British consulates that occurred in the city in previous years. In both of those attacks, the bomber used a bike and tossed an improvised explosive device. The perpetrator's (or perpetrators') vehicle of choice became the central hook of reports on all the bombings. Of course the *Post* called him (or her, or them) the "Bicycle Bomber."[16] Bombs, bicycles, hooded sweatshirts—scary stuff. A report in the *Times* quoted criminal profiler Ray Pierce, who noted that the bomber looked "comfortable" on the bike and therefore could

---

*Many cities have been following the tone set by the NYPD. For example, prior to the Democratic National Convention in August 2008, as freaked-out Denver officials were mistakenly anticipating the influx of fifty thousand bandanna-wearing, window-smashing anarchist demonstrators, the Denver PD issued a "first responder alert" urging public safety personnel of all types to be on the lookout for items they said were often "stockpiled" by these violent protesters. Bicycles were on the list with gas masks, caltrops, and posts with nails sticking out of them. Apparently bicycles and violent anarchy go gloved hand in hand these days in the weird fantasy world of the security bureaucracy.[15]

well be a messenger.[17] This prompted messengers around the world to mumble into their newspapers, "Hey, wait a second there, jackass."

Amazingly, reports did not mention whether or not the Bicycle Bomber was wearing a helmet.*

---

*Since the New York City Bicycle Bomber last struck, there have been a few reports of suicide bombers in Iraq and Afghanistan bicycling to their doomed targets. As time goes on we're bound to hear more and more of these reports of various maniacs and two-bit criminals doing their nefarious business on bikes. Dangerous people become more numerous each day and the bicycle, with its stealth and maneuverability is well suited for many purposes besides commuting or sport.

THE ALIENS

The Flare-Up

IN THE LATE 1960S AND EARLY TO MID-1970S, INTEREST IN bicycling flared up again in the United States like an old campfire that hadn't been properly extinguished. Nobody is exactly sure why it came back or why it came back when it did. It would be convenient for this author if the reemergence of the bicycle at this time could be pinned neatly on the energy crisis of 1973. It would be easy to say that there was an energy crisis, then bingo-bango, people started riding bikes. Unfortunately, the bicycle renaissance seems to have been well under way by the time of the October 1973 Arab-Israeli War, Arab embargo, and subsequent spike in the price of oil. It does seem to be that the embargo had an effect on the Bike Boom, as it's often called, intensifying it and stretching it out for a year or two, but it could not have been the cause. On the other hand there were energy issues mounting before the embargo which could have spurred bike sales—energy prices had been on the rise as the market tightened with the peak in U.S. production and nationalization of Middle Eastern supplies.

Nineteen seventy-three was the best year ever for sales of adult bicycles,[1] although this record would seem to be in jeopardy due to recent trends, if it hasn't been surpassed already. The Bike Boom of the 1970s died like the boom of the 1890s, after hopeful assumptions about continuously growing demand simply failed to materialize. As in the 1890s, the 1970s boom was flattened under car tires. No reports of any suspicious fires.

Reversing the Trans-Atlantic Flow of Style

Pneumatic shoes are worn, it is said, by some bicyclists in Portland, Oregon.

Essex County (N.Y.) Republican, 1897[2]

Not much Lycra in 1973—this was the age of wool. But even then there were the tight black shorts, the one article of clothing that has remained so emblematic of bicycling to Americans.* Little black shorts, and those little cotton

---

*Racers used long, tight shorts continuously from the very early years of the sport. Use of tight black shorts by non-racing bicyclists can be traced well into the nineteenth century and, perhaps fittingly, to France. In September 1893 the *New York Times* reported on a trip to Paris taken by Richard Betts, the president of the Manhattan Bicycling Club, and Isaac Potter. Betts told the paper that "many of the wheelmen ride through the streets of the city with their legs bare from the knee to the ankles, and no one notices it. The men simply say it is cooler. The women all wear bloomer trousers."[3]

caps; many wore them with the tiny bills flipped up. It was a strange look. A fellow dressed like that in 1970s America would have no problem setting himself apart from the crowd. This was before widespread use of helmets. At some point a few folks started wearing those rudimentary helmets composed of padded leather strips—"hairnets." That was the acorn of the mighty oak that is America's helmet dementia. Jerseys, of course. Wool jerseys, tight and colorful, although, generally speaking, not so garish and bright as the jerseys today. The shoes were unmistakably European, and strapped into, onto, and around the pedal with Alfredo Binda straps. Bindas were the best because they didn't stretch and you couldn't get your foot out of them without releasing the buckle. A lot of riders fell over at stoplights then, just as they do today.

The self-imposed predicament of American cycling enthusiasts of the 1970s is represented nicely by Dave Stohler (Dennis Christopher), lead character in the movie *Breaking Away* (1979). *Breaking Away*, by the way, is one of the fine little feel-good movies of the past forty or fifty summers, so rent that sucker or catch it on cable. Barbara Barrie is excellent as Dave's mom. Anyway, Dave Stohler's love of riding was obvious, but that wasn't his only attraction to the machine. He was an awkward kid who used his bicycle to recede from the oppressive mainstream of Bloomington, Indiana. He pretended to be an Italian bike racer—about as un-American a creature as could be imagined by his concerned father. (At one point Dave is seen riding in the draft of a semi at about sixty miles per hour, which is not only un-American but un-possible.*) In Stohler we see a reflection of many American bicyclists of the 1970s and '80s, in love with the machine and yet out of step with society.

Of course, in the end Dave wins the big race, and thus redeems himself for years of acting and dressing so strangely. If he had failed to win, a consortium of concerned friends and family would have had little choice but to strangle him and stash his skinny biker's body at the quarry.

Consciously or not, Dave Stohler and less fictitious American cyclists of the '70s were adopting style elements from European bicycle racing. When Americans start co-opting Euro style points, that's a red flag. All bets are off at that point. The proper flow of style is America-to-Europe, across the Atlantic, eastbound: rhythm and blues, jazz, hip-hop, Levis, Hasselhoff. The Euros and Brits then obsess over and study these various nuggets of style and culture and send them back to us in the form of album-oriented rock bands like the Rolling Stones. "Exile on Main Street" was more American than

---

*Unless your chainring is comically large and has about seventy-five teeth, that is. It is indeed possible to ride in the wake of a large vehicle at such speeds — "Mile-a-Minute" Murphy did it behind a train over one hundred years ago and thus earned his nickname, before crashing heavily into the back of said train — but it requires far more gear inches than were available on Stohler's Masi, and far far more than were available with the smaller of the bike's two chainrings, which the Stohler character was depicted using during his truck chase. Even in bike-centric movies, directors have been unconcerned about providing bike-related authenticity to American audiences. For another example see *Quicksilver* (1986), in which we see a chain shifting in the wrong direction on a sprocket and Kevin Bacon coasting on what is supposed to be a fixed gear. By the way, Mile-a-Minute Murphy, who was entirely authentic, later became a motorcycle cop in New York City, where he smashed his knee in a wreck.[4]

a Chicago-style hot dog. That's the way it's supposed to work. Keith Richards was just channeling the righteous rhythm of the universe. But the American cyclists of the early 1970s turned the natural order upside down and started receiving raw fashion tips not just from Europe but from one of the most obscure facets of the European cultural experience. The predictable result—a cultural abyss opened between the emblematically clad cyclists and the rest of America. To the seeming satisfaction of many of them, the American cyclist of the 1970s was classified as an alien being, and the idea that a special suit is necessary to ride a bike became re-entrenched.

While the number of cycle commuters and casual riders grew, the bicycling that occurred in this period generally perpetuated the bone-deep American bias that regarded the bicycle almost exclusively as go-fast sporting equipment. This was a time when it was re-decided that the proper way for an adult to ride a bike in America was dressed as a bicycle racer, while fantasizing about being one. Indeed, that is one way to do it.

The Bicyclist's Costume

Don't wear a clown's costume. It inspires facetious comment.

"Don'ts for the Wheelman," *Boulder Daily Camera,* 1895[5]

When Frances Willard, the famous women's libber and head of the Women's Christian Temperance Union, geared up to learn how to ride a bicycle, she acquired a steed which she promptly named Gladys. But she knew that there was much more to riding a bike than the bike itself.

"It is needless to say," she explained in a small book about the experience called *Wheel within a Wheel* (1895), "that a bicycling costume was a prerequisite." Ah yes, the bicycling costume. You'll never get fifteen meters without your bicycling costume.

Willard had not yet joined the bloomer revolution. Her costume "consisted of a skirt and blouse of tweed, with belt, rolling collar, and loose cravat, the skirt three inches from the ground; a round straw hat, and walking shoes with gaiters."[6] She is seen in a photo sitting precariously atop what appears to be a Humber ladies' safety, looking quite a bit like an elderly Mary Poppins.

We can't make fun of Willard too exuberantly while dressed in our own bizarre period-piece outfits. Sometimes it seems like the machine itself had been invented just so some dudes could wear particularly unusual outfits that they had conceived but hadn't found any other passable excuse to wear in public. Since the beginning bicycling has been associated with weird outfits—perhaps, more than anything, a testament to the power of marketing departments in the bicycling accessories industry. When the bicycle came back in the 1970s, there was a second chance—to ease up on the manufactured exclusivity, to be less out there, to use clothing that would seem slightly less freakish and alienating to the wider population. It didn't happen, in fact we went the other direction. Since then technology made decked-out bicyclists shiny, too, and marketing departments spawned the insect-head-like bicycle helmet. Bicyclists drifted farther from customary dress.

Bike clothing is a touchy subject among those who wear it. There are a lot of guys out there wearing the gear who know they look a little off, but they're trying to forget about it. They understand that their special costume gets some segment of society all atwitter. They've decided that the practical benefits outweigh the negatives, they're going to wear the clothes, and that's that. They'd rather not discuss it.

And then there are the bicyclists who wear the clothing for reasons having virtually nothing to do with practicality. They dress up in bike clothes so they can feel and look like "real" cyclists, because that's what "real" cyclists wear. A lot of unnecessary leg shaving occurs for this reason as well. There are those who are attracted to the look-at-me factor of a shiny, bright-colored outfit. A lot of bicyclists are self-conscious about their lack of experience and try to cover it up with expensive equipment. You'll never get anybody to admit it, but there are all kinds of cultural and emotional reasons blowing like a tailwind behind the proliferation of bicycle clothing.

Nonetheless, the practical benefits of the clothing are many. First and foremost, the shorts: tight-fitting and now usually made of stretchy, shiny artificial fabrics. Generally black, thankfully—bright-colored bicycle shorts are a special abomination. Most of these shorts have a piece of soft fabric sewn into the crotch. The tight fit is much more aerodynamic than, say, a pair of cargo shorts (wind drag is a surprisingly significant consideration for the bicyclist) and it cuts down on chafing. The shorts are built for comfort but they are also constricting in ways that some men may find very uncomfortable. The jerseys are likewise aerodynamic, with fabrics engineered to keep the skin dry. Zippers and pockets placed just so after a hundred-year evolution of the garment. Special hats and shoes and socks. Even the bright colors can be useful in traffic. But none of it is remotely necessary for normal everyday riding. And nothing about it is so important that bicyclists need to inflict their tightly wrapped forms upon the other patrons at the Starbucks.

Some go so far as to say they would never ride without their bike clothes—the "kit" is too comfortable and important, so immensely practical that it's indispensable. But a lot of the people making these claims have never really tried to ride in their normal clothes. They bought the gear when they bought the bike, as Frances Willard did. They came into it with the assumption, which they picked up somewhere like a bad cold, that special clothes were a necessary part of the deal. How many folks want to dress up like a shiny superhero when they go about their daily business? The mistaken assumption that such a costume is necessary equipment remains one of the most persistent obstacles to wider adoption of the bicycle for everyday transportation purposes.

CHALLENGES OF THE WHEEL.

Willard's Wobbles

At first she will be upset by the apparition of the smallest poodle, and not until she has attained a wide experience will she hold herself steady in presence of a coach with four horses.

Frances Willard, 1895[1]

THE IDEAL BICYCLING COSTUME FOR FRANCES WILLARD WOULD have included some kind of old-fashioned elbow and knee pads, frankly.

Willard was a friend of Albert Pope. In the days before she learned to ride a two-wheeler, the Colonel presented her with one of his company's Columbia tricycles, not unlike the one Hiram Maxim customized to create one of the world's first motor vehicles. On her first ride on this trike, she pedaled furiously, joyously, and overcooked a turn. She rolled it and smashed her elbow, and the injury was serious enough to require minor surgery. She had this to say about her experience under the ether: "It let me out into a new world, greater, more mellow, more god-like, and it did me no harm at all."[2] Frances Willard, leader of the Women's Christian Temperance Union and crusader against inebriation, likes getting loaded. Check.

Later, when she was learning to ride her two-wheeler Gladys, she fell badly and bashed her knee, illustrating one of the inescapable aspects of the machine. The same feature that leads to a glorious sense of flight when everything is going well also causes the occasional topple when trouble arises. Those who really love to ride don't like that fact about bicycling, but they won't denounce the trade-off. They know there's no other way. Freedom, as they say, is not free. In the case of some novice riders who are particularly unsteady or stiff, the topples may be more frequent, and more damaging. Bicycling demands coordination, fluidity of motion, and quickness of reflexes far beyond what is necessary for driving. It takes extra-special skill to dump a tricycle.

Willard combined her unusual wobbliness with a certain strength of spirit. Despite her pulverized elbow, surgery, and bashed knee, she retained her desire to learn how to ride on two wheels. She persisted and found that the rewards overwhelmed even these painful crash experiences. Eventually, the wobble went away.

Bicycling requires a certain minimal sum of skill and spirit. If you're low on the skill, like Willard was when she began, you need to be strong in other ways to make up for it.

It turns out that bicycling is a unique activity that isn't for everybody, and that's okay.

Fear Itself

The only thing we have to fear is fear itself.

FDR, 1933[3]

FDR was completely, utterly wrong about that. Totally, massively wrong.

The famous line is from his inauguration speech of 1933. The country had tumbled into the economic abyss, and Roosevelt was telling us, "Hey, we'll get through this if we just buckle down. Stop panicking." He was also saying, "Hey, don't pay too close attention to the man behind the curtain there as he goes completely bonkers on the levers of power for a few years." Of course, the record shows that within a decade of FDR's reassurance and, some might say, puffery, the whole world had gone to hell. As a result of the Great Depression that we weren't supposed to fear, a bunch of lunatic fascists had taken over Europe and much of Asia and had the bright idea to dominate the entire world with an iron fist or, failing that, take everyone down with them in a giant ball of fire, kamikaze style. When I think of the phrase "nothing to fear," the first thing that pops into my mind is not the German Nazi industrial machine working feverishly to produce atomic weapons.

Fear itself, eh? Tell it to the guys who were on the USS *Indianapolis,* or the ones who took the beach on Iwo Jima, running from crater to crater on the black sand scattered with the body parts of their fellow soldiers. The people of Guernica, Dresden, Tokyo, Stalingrad. Six million Jews. Let's be frank, Franklin. When you said that, there was plenty more to fear out there than just fear. Fire-bombing, holocausts and dismemberment. The proper response to your statement would have been a hearty *Ha!*

In hindsight we can say that FDR was sugarcoating it. It's like when dentists decorate their waiting rooms with pastel prints of children and kittens having picnics, to keep their patients' minds off the fact that they're about to get bloody mouth-jousted with industrial drills. In my view that just makes it worse. I'd rather get prepared with some Hieronymous Bosch. Maybe a little Goya action—paint *Saturn Eating His Children* directly on the waiting-room wall.

Bicycle advocacy has been marked by the tendency to deemphasize, if not outright sugarcoat, the level of danger faced by bicyclists on the streets. The tendency to sugarcoat is driven by the perception, held by many advocates, that there are all these would-be bicyclists out there who have an inkling to ride but choose not to out of an irrational fear of getting run down by a car. There's some truth in the perception. Non-bicyclists often express the opinion that bicyclists must be crazy to brave traffic, and from some semi-official corners—advocates of mandatory helmet laws, opponents of public programs aimed at increasing ridership, for instance—there have indeed been wacky exaggerations of the danger.

When people say that bicycling is dangerous, it sounds like an attack, or an excuse, to many advocates, and it usually is one of those things. So they dig into the available statistics to show that bicycling is a relatively safe activity, something that they already believe quite strongly. But when they open up the data, all sorts of bats and unidentified creatures fly out. Ken Kifer, for instance, was very interested in highlighting the safety of cycling on his extensive and informative Web site, to combat what he felt were irrational fears. So he presented a survey to his readers to gather information on patterns of use and frequency of injury. Kifer expressed a good deal of surprise when his data showed that bicycling was nineteen to thirty-three times more likely to result in injury than driving a car the same distance.* And then, in a horrible lightning flash of tragedy, Kifer himself was killed by a drunk driver while riding his bicycle.

If the non-cycling population's suspicion that bicycling is relatively dangerous turns out to be correct—to the chagrin of many cycling advocates—the nature of the danger still remains badly misunderstood. Contrary to popular belief, and

---

*The bicyclist fares quite a bit better on a per-hour basis, but still faces elevated risk with respect to drivers.[4] Kifer is to be commended for publishing data that contradicted his stated assumptions and biases. His survey was very small in scope and questionable for several reasons, but the results are corroborated—as much as anything has ever been corroborated in the imperfect world of accident statistics and surveys—by much more involved research projects. The average accident rate of Kifer's respondents was quite close to that recorded by William Moritz in his very large survey of League of American Bicyclists members.[5] In both surveys the average respondent was a relatively experienced bicyclist (approximately fourteen years) who rode a few thousand miles per year with about a 10 percent chance of suffering some notable injury in any given year; although their injury rates were elevated with respect to those in cars, the rates were far better than rates that have been recorded for novice bicyclists and children. Such surveys, while inherently unscientific, are also about as scientific as it gets when it comes to accident and injury statistics.[6]

with respect to people like Ken Kifer who have been tragically killed by them, bicyclists' elevated injury rate has relatively little to do with cars and their incompetent drivers. The extra risk is largely explained by the unique challenges involved in operating a two-wheel in-line vehicle—namely, wiping out, smashing into things, and falling over, even when there are no cars in sight. Bicycling and driving are radically different activities. Bicyclists must contend with a large number of factors that drivers don't need to consider, in particular many different types of road damage, debris, and surface anomalies. You can smack into a little pothole when you're not ready for it and crash. Go around a corner too fast and wipe out on some sand. Wet railroad tracks become treacherous obstacles. Seemingly tiny cracks can displace the front wheel. Such things comprise the extra danger of bicycling. Among the million bicyclists who show up at emergency rooms or doctor's offices seeking treatment for bicycle-related injuries every year, only about 15 percent are there because of collisions with cars.*

The injuries that result from the bicyclist's failure to stay upright can be quite serious, even deadly on rare occasions if

---

*This is an estimate derived from estimates of the number of bicyclists injured in collisions with motor vehicles (see Halleyesus, Annest, and Dellinger, "Cyclists injured while sharing the road with motor vehicles," *Injury Prevention,* June 2007, 202-6) and estimates of total numbers of bicyclists seeking medical treatment given by the United States Consumer Product Safety Commission's National Electronic Injury Surveillance System (NEISS), a statistical sampling from a network of emergency rooms around the country. The NEISS estimates that approximately a half million bicyclists show up at emergency departments and another half million at doctor's offices annually due to bicycling accidents.

the head smacks the ground hard enough. In general, however, these injuries tend to remain in the range from superficial bumps and scrapes to collarbone fractures. The more serious the cyclist's injury, the more likely that it was caused by a collision with a motor vehicle. At the bottom of the bicyclists' injury pyramid we find a high number of minor injuries—millions annually—relatively few of them caused by collisions. At the top it's exactly the opposite: relatively few serious injuries, the vast majority of which result from collisions. And when a bicyclist is killed, it's almost always due to getting hit or, quite literally, run over.

It's true that bicyclists get squeezed from both sides. They are more likely to be injured due to the difficulties involved in the actual act of riding, and also more likely to be seriously hurt in a collision should one occur. After all, how many of the tens of thousands of bicyclists injured in collisions every year have a corresponding injured driver? Approaching zero. Nationally, bicyclists make up about 2 percent of all traffic fatalities but nowhere near that share of road users. But we need to keep things in perspective. Neither the bicyclist nor the driver is in imminent danger of being snuffed out. It's likely that the fatality rate for bicyclists is higher than the rate for drivers, but the fatality rate for each activity is, well, I'm not going to call it astronomically low, because that would be an unnecessary jinx, but it's low, on the order of one per million hours. (The driver's extra protection is canceled at least somewhat by his or her capacity to travel at much higher speeds than the bicyclist, so while the driver's injury rate is far lower, the fatality rates begin to converge.) This already low rate should be considered in light of the fact that it is an average for the entire population of riders, a population that includes little kids and drunks and people who careen around wildly in the middle of the night in dark clothing. The per-hour accident and fatality rates seen here are quite a bit worse than what we would see from a hypothetical population consisting only of smart, careful adult riders* (keeping in mind that Kifer was a smart and careful rider, and it didn't help him any).

It is an undeniable truth that the bicyclist is more vulnerable to injury than the driver, but it is not reasonable to be paranoid about bicycling in traffic and then to climb into an auto without a second thought. Such cognitive dissonance is another symptom of our national sickness.

Safety in Numbers

Both Fear and Safety lurk in the dark forests of the accident statistics. Something large and carnivorous is crunching through the underbrush in the dark. But what's that over there—a sunny clearing. Wildflowers waving in the breeze. Ah, that looks inviting. I think I'll go over there.

---

*We must remember as well that the tally for bicyclists is massively skewed by the inclusion of children. The portion of child victims among all bicyclist fatalities has fallen like a stone for over thirty years, from about two thirds in 1975 to less than one fifth in 2006, reflecting the continuing loss of the bicycle's popularity among kids.[7]

The sunny clearing of the bicycling-related statistical forest is the Safety in Numbers theory. In 2003 Peter Jacobsen published a study of accident statistics and census numbers from sixty-eight cities in California, as well as multiple countries, showing a strong correlation between collision rates and the numbers of people riding bikes or walking in those cities. Jacobsen showed that greater numbers of cycle commuters (he used census figures for cycle commuting) on the streets are associated with a lower probability of car-bicycle collision. Cities with very low numbers of bike commuters might also show low numbers of collisions, but the rate of collisions per rider or collisions per mile would be significantly higher than the rates seen in a city like Davis, with its relative throngs of commuters on wheels.

To explain the happy correlation, Jacobsen unleashed some sweeping assumptions. He writes: "Since it is unlikely that the people walking and bicycling become more cautious if their numbers are larger, it indicates that the behavior of motorists controls the likelihood of collisions with people walking and bicycling. It appears that motorists adjust their behavior in the presence of people walking and bicycling."[8] The theory being that drivers get used to seeing more of these "vulnerable road users" out there, begin to expect them, perhaps on a subconscious level, and tone down their driving accordingly. It's a seductive line of thought that would seem to explain quite a lot while promising easy answers for the future. Why isn't bicycling safe? Not enough bicyclists. How do we make bicycling safer? Just attract more bicyclists. Easy breezy.

A little too easy, of course. Jacobsen's numerical analysis was solid, but the theory that followed from it was just that. Jacobsen notes that changes in either bicyclist or driver behavior must account for the wide variation in collision rates, and states that "it is unlikely that the people walking and bicycling become more cautious if their numbers are larger." He doesn't offer any support for this assumption. But cities with greater numbers of cycle commuters—the parameter recorded by Jacobsen—do in fact have different bicycling populations than cities with few cycle commuters. Bicycle commuters tend to be among the most careful and conservative riders. Where there are lots of bike commuters, there are lots of conscientious and relatively experienced riders. The total population of cyclists in these communities would also include children, drunks, and various other disasters-on-wheels, but the ratio of careful riders to reckless ones will be higher where there are significant numbers of cycle commuters. And accident rates in these places would be relatively low.

When Jacobsen counted total car-bike collisions from police reports, he included an unknown number of incidents involving children under sixteen. In doing so he makes the oldest and most common mistake in the book when it comes to analyzing bicycle safety. These days kids are involved in about 15 percent of bicyclist fatalities and injuries. It used to be much higher. Just fifteen or so years ago, the kids' share of bicyclists' traffic fatalities was about one-third; in 1975 kids under sixteen accounted for two-thirds of the deaths, indicating a sharp drop in the number of kids on bikes since then.[9] When we look at accident statistics over time and see that the number of riders has gone up while the accident rate has gone down, we have to keep in mind that the relative share of kid bicyclists has likely been declining sharply over the same period. Thus, the population of cyclists has actually become more careful and conservative overall, by default. And when we compare different locales, as Jacobsen did, and see that cities with more commuters have lower accident rates, keep in mind that the average bicyclist there could simply be a better, smarter (and older) rider than the average bicyclist somewhere else, contrary to Jacobsen's assumption.

The experience of motorcyclists also casts doubt on the notion of Safety in Numbers. Motorcycling skyrocketed in popularity over the past decade, and motorbike registrations actually doubled between 2000 and 2005. Over the same period the ratio of fatalities to registrations held steady. The fatality-per-mile rate has nearly doubled since 1996, with vastly more total miles ridden now.[10]

The pattern of motorcycle accidents and fatalities is somewhat different than the pattern we see in the bicycle world. A slight majority of motorcyclist fatalities are caused by collisions or interactions with cars, while the vast majority of bicyclist deaths result from collisions. The typical bicyclist is much less likely to die in traffic than the typical motorcyclist, although the bicyclist is more likely to be injured in some piddly solo wreck. Still, on their low-profile vehicles motorcyclists face many of the same issues faced by bicyclists. Both should be considered "vulnerable road users"—under constant threat of being overlooked by drivers and pedestrians and then exposed to greater injury than drivers should a collision occur. But the whole Safety in Numbers thing isn't working out very well for the motorcyclists. Drivers don't seem to be any better at noticing them even though their numbers have gone way up.

People mine the stats in search of what they need to hear. Bicyclists have been searching feverishly for shiny nuggets and coming up with lumps of coal. The accident numbers are depressingly non-reassuring. So when Jacobsen's Safety in Numbers came along, people latched onto it as if it were the last gold nugget in the whole valley. The paper has been cited by dozens of others since it appeared in 2003, and its central assumption has been endorsed without reservation. There has been undeniable enthusiasm for it.[11] I believe the theory has a twofold attraction. First, it seems to provide a singular simple answer to many questions of bicycle advocacy, and everybody loves easy answers; second, and probably more important, the theory sneakily transfers the responsibility for the bicyclist's well-being from the bicyclist to the driver. It is the driver, Jacobsen says, who "controls the likelihood of collision." Many bicyclists seem to shrink from the responsibility for their own safety, and what a relief Jacobsen's conclusion is to those people. It's exactly what they want to believe.

The truth remains that the "control" lies substantially with the bicyclists, whether they want it or not. Any experienced rider will tell you that.

The New Potters

They that know nothing fear nothing.

Frances Willard, 1895[12]

Isaac Potter, the guy who wanted bicycles to be classified with carriages under the law, certainly seems like a nineteenth-century sort of character—I like to imagine him in a woolen uniform and with a big mustache—but there are Potters among us still. Among present-day bicyclists Potter has a scattering of ideological soul brothers who call themselves the Vehicular Cyclists. The Vehicular Cyclist motto is "Bicyclists fare best when they act and are treated as drivers of vehicles."[13] The vehicles have changed quite a bit since Potter's "Liberty Law," but the fundamental trade-off remains intact: Bicyclists will be subject to vehicular law and in this they will secure access, while at the same time some of what can be done with a bike in city traffic, some of what the bicycle is, will be denied. According to the VCers, the payoff in respect is well worth the cost in freedom of movement.

The suspiciously polished slogan, and much of the Vehicular Cyclist official lexicon, comes from John Forester, the Burl Ives–looking figurehead of upright, "competent" cycling for the twentieth century. Knowing as we do about fellows from the musty past like Isaac Potter, it's difficult to endorse Forester as the father of the vehicular movement, but he is the one who started banging the VC war drum in the 1970s in response to the modern Bike Boom and the concurrent emphasis of government planning agencies on creating separate facilities for bicyclists. Forester's crusade has always been directed primarily at bike lanes and the idea that bicyclists should be "shoved over to the side" (as he puts it) to make way for motor traffic. The anti–bike lane crusade puts Forester and his followers squarely at odds with the majority of bicycling advocacy organizations in the country, none of which include in their mission statements a desire to shove anyone to the side, mind you, but which nonetheless like to lobby for the creation of new bike lanes and various other sorts of bicycle facilities.

Channeling Isaac Potter, Forester helped enact laws all over the country that ensured access to certain roads and enhanced bicyclists' rights. In general, bicyclists are required by law to stay "as far right as practicable" on any road they're using. This means that in the presence of faster traffic bicyclists are supposed to move right to enable a pass—but Forester and the VCs helped define this queer word "practicable," a strange legalese, in the bicyclists' favor, winning special dispensation for bicyclists to "take the lane" should any one of a long list of conditions be present.* Forester's incessant complaining about the poor design of some bike facilities has spurred improvement in those facilities.

---

*Typically, a bicyclist is allowed use of the full lane if he or she judges the lane is too narrow to allow safe passing, if the bicyclist is traveling the same speed as motor traffic, or in the presence of road damage or other surface factors that the bicyclist deems too dangerous to negotiate. In other words, it's largely left to the discretion of the rider. This is one of the murkiest, least-well-known traffic laws on the books.

Who's to say where bicycling would be in this country without the likes of Potter and Forester? It's conceivable that bicyclists could have been banished from the roads at some point. The opponents of Forester would have a chuckle at the notion that he saved us from any such fate. Many would argue that Forester has been a force in opposition to the general advancement of bicycling and bicyclists' rights, that we'd all be better off without him. The word "obstructionist" will come out. Due to his association with a group called the American Dream Coalition, which seems to exist to promote the very idea of automobile-based suburban development, some observers have actually accused Forester of being a shill for automotive interests, a mole sent to ruin bicycling advocacy from the inside. (The charge seems unlikely, although Forester is listed on the speakers list for the ADC, and his picture appears on their Web site, www.americandreamcoalition.org.)

Forester has been fighting his war for almost forty years, and he's attracted quite a crowd of opponents, some of whom have been bickering with him for about that long. His most bitter antagonists are of course other bicycling advocates. Forester was president of the League of American Wheelmen in the 1970s, but split nastily from LAW when they started leaning in favor of the dreaded bikeways. The split has festered over the decades with nasty backbiting soap opera drama. Unnoticed by factions on both sides, the object of their disagreement passed into obsolescence.

The Sharrow Revolution

Lines on the street. That's what it's all about to some people.

An outsider looking in on the weird world of bicycling advocacy and policy—checking out the Internet back-and-forth and conferences and public works initiatives—might get the mistaken impression that the issue of bike lanes is highly important. Opposing camps of advocates have formed and their positions have ossified and splinter groups have splintered and feelings have been hurt, and, I'd wager, lawsuits have been filed, all over lines on the street.

Unlike the groups whose members have been apoplectic about bike lanes for decades, and unlike John Forester, the figurehead of the anti–bike lane caucus who steers every discussion to the evil of "bikeways," most highly experienced traffic cyclists don't get too excited about bike lanes at all. To a good rider even the worst bike lane ranks somewhere between an annoyance and a curiosity. Some of the separate facilities created for bicyclists can properly be called dangerous and should be avoided regardless of the law, but a good rider will have little problem dealing even with these. So it's difficult to get them riled up about the threat that bike lanes pose to civilization.

I had an interesting experience with a new bike lane in Denver. For a dozen years or more, I had traveled a westbound thoroughfare downtown called 18th Street. It was a busy street without any sort of bike accommodation. Literally tens of thousands of times I had pedaled down 18th. Then one day a bike lane was placed on the street. It was an extremely stellar bike lane of luxurious width—perhaps eight feet across.* There was side parking on 18th, but this bike lane was placed, in its entirety, well outside the "door zone." That is, the right line of the bike lane was about five or six feet to the left of the door handles of the parked cars. This highly unusual degree of spatial luxury was achieved the only way possible, by removing the rightmost of the four travel lanes on 18th. It would be almost impossible to create a better bike lane than this. Indeed, this is perhaps the finest example of a bike lane that I have ever seen in my life. And yet I couldn't help noticing that the addition of this feature had no effect whatsoever on my rides down 18th. None.

If bike lanes don't really do anything, then why are they so popular? Bike lanes have two main advantages. First, they are cheap. Throw down some paint, nothing to it. This allows traffic engineers and planners to make a visible impact and, in their minds, promote bicycle transportation and livable communities and all that without much cost at all. In that regard bike lanes are tremendously attractive. Their second big advantage is that novice riders really like the idea. New or prospective transportational bicyclists often mention the presence or absence of bicycle lanes as a make-or-break factor in their decision to ride or not, so those who want to bring

---

*Strangely, people have a difficult time estimating the width of surface features like bike lanes and sidewalks. Seven feet is quite wide for a bike lane, but most people would look at it and say it's five or six feet wide. It doesn't look as wide somehow when looking at it from above. What looks like four and a half feet to most people is actually about six feet; what looks like eight feet is ten. This is possibly due to humans' exaggerated perception of their own stature.

increasing numbers of riders onto the streets see a straight line through bike lanes to their goal. A bike lane could also be helpful in encouraging rogue bicyclists to ride in the street, rather than on the sidewalk. The critics jump in and say the lines give novice riders an unjustified sense of security that actually increases risk. There isn't much statistical evidence to support such assertions, or the assertions of the pro–bike lane crowd, for that matter.

Thankfully the bike lane "controversy" is obsolete, because bike lanes are obsolete. The transportation planner who still thinks in terms of lines is a dinosaur. Wake up, fella. A new surface treatment is proliferating that carries most of the advantages of bike lanes without the controversial disadvantages. The sharrow. It sounds like something Bruce and Demi would name their kid. A sharrow is a graphic surface treatment either painted or placed on the street. It portrays the simple graphic form of a bicycle inside or on top of a large arrow or chevron, alerting drivers that the road should be shared with bicyclists: the shared-use arrow. Because it clearly signals that the bicyclist's place is in the street (a message for bicyclists as well as drivers), but doesn't keep the bicyclist confined to an area of the street where he can be more vulnerable, the sharrow is the new best in class among surface treatments for bicyclists.

There are some sharrow pitfalls that need to be avoided. These fall into two general categories: making the sharrow too small and putting it too far to the right. Either mistake will neutralize the marking's effectiveness. The original versions of the sharrow, created decades ago by Denver's bicycle coordinator, James Mackay, were quite small, just a few feet across, and were placed right where the right-side tires of cars tended to track. Within a few months of their installation, the Denver markings were beaten into submission. They virtually disappeared. Other sharrows were placed inside bike lanes, which is nearly useless. You might as well put a stencil of a banana in there. Denver's sharrows at once introduced the concept and displayed several examples of what not to do with them.

Mackay's sharrow graphic made its way to cities around the nation and started to evolve. Bike-lane-loving San Francisco experimented with different styles of markings and found that a more refined-looking double-chevron design was most effective in changing driver and bicyclist behavior.[14] Installing the markers was a natural step for San Francisco's bike planners, as it allowed them to encourage bicyclists zooming down the city's infamous hills to move farther away from right-side hazards than bike lanes had previously allowed. Visiting Santa Fe in the spring of 2008, I saw something beautiful. Not a sunset or a kachina doll, but very large sharrows placed right in the middle of the travel lanes on some streets. There wasn't too much transportational bicycling going on in Santa Fe, but the streets were beckoning. Several months later I was encouraged to see new, much larger, and more sharply stylized sharrows being placed on several streets of my hometown. The "Denver arrows" were back home and all grown up. They were like the original Mackay sharrows on steroids—sharroids—and they were being placed well out into the lane in most cases.

As with bike lanes, sharrows don't provide any physical protection against cars running you over. There's no force field there. But they do affect the riding environment in real, positive ways that are hard to explain. In sharp contrast to the bike lanes, I sensed an obvious and most welcome difference after the prominent new-generation sharrow markings were put down. The San Francisco sharrow study showed that the markings affected motorists' position on the road, when passing bicyclists and even when no bicyclists were present; they altered their position by a foot or two, a significant amount in the eyes of a bicyclist on the typical city street, but there's something else going on with the sharrows that's impossible to quantify. Imagine if the word SLOW were painted on the street. Just because a driver sees the word doesn't mean he'll slow down. But he's more likely to slow down, and even if he doesn't he'll likely be thinking about why the word is there—he'll be more aware. He may even be a little confused, and that's good. The same goes for the sharrow. The sharrow doesn't really tell the bicyclist or the driver to do anything specifically, and therein lies much of its beauty. It's art that conjures awareness, and that, as we've seen, is what traffic safety is all about. It makes people think. The sharrow serves the additional purpose of preemptively calming motorists who would otherwise be predisposed to becoming agitated at or aggressive toward any bicyclist they find in their way. The sharrows are undeniable in their message, even to people who can't read: The road doesn't belong just to cars. The bicyclist has a right to be there after all—if you run him down, you'll get in trouble. To some this comes as quite an eye-opener.

Sharrows really seem to work. I suppose there is some danger that sharrows could be abused, their effect diluted through overuse. Ah heck, put them everywhere, and make them frighteningly large.

Baggage

Most people who ride bikes in America don't do it with a thought in their head about subverting the power structure, attacking oppressive traditions, or making any kind of statement whatsoever about anything. They are not concerned in the slightest with the bicycle as idea. They don't think much of the sociological, historical, or even ecological implications of the ride. They certainly aren't on their way to a bombing. These folks are into the bicycle as machine alone, and they don't sense any void left by their lack of appreciation for the many other sociopolitical aspects of its short history.

In the United States about 80 percent of people who ride bikes say they do so for the purpose of pure recreation.[15] And why the hell not? The unique sensation of riding a bike is a powerful intoxicant. That's what hooked Americans on bicycling 120 years ago and it's what keeps us coming back. The thrill of balance that turned and dumped Frances Willard on her kneecap. The simple fun of bicycling has fueled a $6 billion/year industry in the United States.[16]

Fun is apolitical. Fun has no agenda, other than to make you smile. And yet even the person who climbs onto a bike for the simple purpose of having fun or getting a whiff of fresh air will be saddled with the baggage of history, accompanied by a cloud of suspicion hanging around a machine that has at various times been intimately associated with women's liberation, white power, political sneakiness, Asian communism, sabotage and spying and other rebel mischief, the Viet Cong, European socialism, illegal immigrants, serial drunk drivers, anarchy, privilege, anti-car fanaticism, and multiple manifestations of youthful antiestablishment activism. This mishmash of historical symbolism is now woven into the collective subconscious of the nation. The bicycle is loaded.

It's really quite silly that the act of bicycling for transportation has become so politicized in the United States. And it's a bit of a wonder that it's been filed under L for "liberal leftist loon," because bicycling is in fact the most conservative of all vehicles—using one man's definition of conservative anyway. Who knows what conservative is anymore? Some of the people who call themselves conservative make a mockery of the concept, unilaterally invading countries and throwing trillions of public dollars to private enterprise. Perhaps even the Bicycle Bomber can be considered conservative these days.

In transportation, there's nothing more conservative than traveling under your own power. This is the transportation version of living within one's means, the guiding directive of the fiscal conservative.

Resentment

For some reason or another in years past there was a prejudice against the bicycle. The high wheels were said to be dangerous, and when the speedy-geared safeties were introduced they were not taken too kindly. Now, however, all is changed. The prejudice has been removed and a man can mount a machine and pedal through the toughest of localities without fear of being molested by street arabs and called a dude.

New York Times, 1894[17]

The baggage of history makes it slightly more difficult to ride the streets, and becomes another barrier in the way of widespread adoption of the machine for utilitarian purposes. Every time bicycling becomes associated with another cause, whether it be legit or wacko, right or left, more people are alienated from it than attracted to it.

But bicyclists don't need to associate themselves with any cause to sow resentment and repel the populace. Many people are angered by bicyclists because they see them as a bunch of scofflaws who do as they please in traffic, ignoring lights and stop signs, scaring old ladies and kittens, while at the same time demanding special treatment and raising holy Cain at the first sign of any violation of the bicyclist's precious space. Motorists commonly express annoyance at the cyclist's perceived sense of entitlement. Some of this sort of anti-bicyclist sentiment is Bike Envy, a longing for the freedom that the bicyclist flaunts; and some is "modism," a natural hatred reflexively expressed by drivers against bicyclists, pedestrians, riders on the bus, anybody not in a car, and returned in kind. Some commuters burst forth with anger against anyone who delays them for a moment. Bicyclists make it even easier for drivers to harbor prejudice against them when they wear equipment and clothing that makes them appear comical, foreign, shiny, and nonhuman.

But some of the anti-bicyclist sentiment is deserved. I say this as a long-time bike guy. Bicyclists have a tendency to, first of all, break laws and take liberties that the brilliant machine makes possible, that's true; on the other hand, they tend to be quite defensive about their personal space in traffic. Slight encroachments are met with, at the least, glares and indignation. It's not so much the lawbreaking or the indignation but the combo of the two that does it. To the motorist it can appear bratty, selfish, and hypocritical.

There are some legitimate reasons, among the duds, for motorists to resent bicyclists, but there are also reasons for bicyclists acting the way they do. Bad driving is more than an annoyance; it's a direct threat to a bicyclist's well-being. If they get tapped by some car, there could be serious consequences. It's not like being in a car. So it's natural for a bicyclist to get all snarly about his or her space out there. Typically a few years of experience will leave the rider with a more stoic demeanor.

Widespread resentment against adult bicyclists is now entering its third successive century. In the summer of 2008, the human incarnation of that resentment was a San Francisco blogger named Rob Anderson. Mr. Anderson channeled an intense distaste, let's call it, for cyclists, derived originally from a close call or two on the street, into a run for local office and a successful lawsuit against the city that stopped the entire S.F. bicycle program in its tracks. "Regardless of the obvious dangers," he writes, "some people will ride bikes in San Francisco for the same reason Islamic fanatics will engage in suicide bombings—because they are politically motivated to do so." To Anderson the bicycle is the strongest symbol of a "progressive movement" that he hates. His successful gumming up of the public works made him a mildly heroic figure to some. He was featured on the front page of the *Wall Street Journal*; CNN's Glenn Beck put him on television and told him to "keep fighting the good fight."[18]

Anderson is not alone. Over the past decade or so, it's become standard fare for shock-jock morning show radio hosts, the barometers of mass sentiment, to verbally attack bicyclists for the amusement of their audiences. Among this crowd bicyclists, especially those in Lycra outfits, are held at about the same level of esteem as Congress, France, or OPEC.

Bicyclists were rightfully up in arms during the summer of 2003, after DJs at stations in Cleveland, Raleigh, and Houston took their antipathy a few steps too far, urging their listeners to perpetrate various acts of violence and harassment against bicyclists. All three stations were owned by Clear Channel Communications, a fact the company insisted was pure coincidence. (This is believable, simply because Clear Channel owns an obscene percentage of the radio stations in the United States.) Through the tyrannical magic of the Inter-

Web, bicyclists nationwide waged a campaign of complaint against Clear Channel that, combined with formal protests to the FCC and the revolt of some advertisers, convinced the company to take action. The DJs were forced into on-air clarifications, regrets, and apologies, and Clear Channel threw some cash at bike safety programs and aired public service announcements.[19] In February 2005, however, a DJ at Sacramento's KTSE suggested violence against bicyclists, and the cycle repeated.

Although it is the first instinct of some to dismiss Anderson and the Clear Channel jocks as isolated, insignificant cranks and jokesters, the sad fact is that their attitude toward bicyclists is not out of step with the mainstream. It is useless for bicyclists to knock themselves out trying to accommodate or mollify non-bicyclists who hold unreasonable or just plain ignorant notions of what bicycling is about. At the same time bicyclists would do well to understand the appeal of their expressions of resentment.

Myth of the Scofflaw Cyclist

Although it may be obsolete in a world of righteous sharrows, there is certainly a kernel or two of truth in Forester's criticism of bike lanes. In his zeal to discredit separate facilities, however, he crafted an argument that mischaracterizes the big picture of bicycling in a few very important ways.

Under Forester's direction the novice bicyclist is encouraged to think of traffic as a fundamentally trustworthy system, a freestanding and self-contained rhythmic condition not unlike the Pythagorean Music of the Spheres. The cyclist is simply to plug himself or herself into this preexisting system and the system itself will act as caretaker over the cyclist's well-being. The possibility of system breakdown is acknowledged but maintained to be remote.[20]

The traffic system, of course, is nowhere near that reliable. Not the system I'm familiar with, anyway. The Forester line shows little appreciation for the fact that traffic is nothing but humans, and glosses over the realities of the danger in riding a bike around so many other humans making typical human mistakes. Emphasizing the abstract system above all else, Vehicular Cycling doesn't do much to help beginners understand the things that are, in my opinion, even more important to a rider's safety than following laws. As a messenger, a job that necessitates breaking traffic laws to satisfy the unholy demands of desperate customers, one unavoidably comes to an understanding that a bicyclist's safety is very much dependent on awareness, and not so much dependent on adherence to traffic code. If it were the other way around, all the messengers would be dead. Experienced messengers are likely to be plenty scarred up, but in fact they compile per-hour injury rates that are orders of magnitude lower than typical cycle commuters or recreational riders. Thus a working messenger can run a hundred or so red lights per shift, shift after shift, for years without ever getting hit or hitting anybody, and without causing chaos, destruction, or panic—then get run over while riding in a completely lawful, yet somewhat absentminded fashion on the way home. It's about awareness.

Accident statistics back this up as well. We occasionally hear that bicyclists are most often found at fault in their collisions with cars, a pronouncement that makes drivers as well as law-abiding bicyclists feel better about life and themselves. However, it is only when looking at the entire population of bicyclists (which, unlike the driver population, includes kids younger than sixteen) that the statement holds true. When adult bicyclists are involved in collisions with motor vehicles, the driver of the car or truck is more likely than the bicyclist to be found at fault. In other words, not only do adult bicyclists still get hit while abiding the law, they may be just as likely, if not more likely, to get hit while following the law than while breaking it. Riding according to the law is clearly not the magic ring that some believe it to be. These crash reports are simply telling us that avoiding collisions is a more complex endeavor than merely plugging into the system.*

Scofflaw bicycling can end badly, but its risks have been

---

*For instance, "serious injury crash factors" were assigned to drivers at a rate of almost three to one over bicyclists in car-bike collisions in New York City from 1996 to 2005.[21] Most studies of populations of bicyclists are heavily weighted with child victims who are very likely to be found at fault in the collisions in which they're involved. Ken Cross's 1974 study of 384 car-bike accidents that occurred in Santa Barbara still provides perhaps the clearest illustration of the nuclear-bomb effect that child bicyclists have on accident studies. Cross found that "there is indeed an interaction between age and accident type and that the interaction is a very significant one." He presented a graph which, as he says, "shows that the age distribution varies widely from accident type to accident type, and furthermore, shows that the distributions tend to fall into two distinct groups. It will be noted that all of the accidents in which the critical maneuver was performed by the bicyclists are clustered together, whereas, all of the accidents in which the critical maneuver was performed by the motorists are also closely clustered." With the given distribution, if the collisions of child bicyclists are culled from the mix, the remaining incidents are predominantly the fault of the motorist.[22] Children are much less likely to ride bicycles than they have been in decades past, but they still tend to comprise a disproportionately large subset of injured bicyclists in accident surveys.

consistently overblown. It's actually more likely that the crunched adult bicyclist will be riding to code prior to the incident, not improvising. Remove the collisions involving child bicyclists and drunken bicyclists—24 percent of bicyclists killed in 2006 were legally intoxicated, according to the Insurance Institute for Highway Safety[23] —and we find a definite theme, a lot of lawful riders getting smacked in much the same way. Such collisions tend to take place at the untimely concurrence of two conditions—the driver's overlooking the bicyclist and the bicyclist's failing to prepare for it. Cluelessness meets innocence on the streets of America.

It's relatively easy for drivers to notice bicyclists riding in the same direction on the same street in front of them, they have the target directly in their line of sight for a relatively long period of time. But drivers have a much tougher time seeing bicyclists (and motorcyclists and scooters, for that matter) when the drivers are endeavoring to make left turns or right turns, bolt across streets, or exit driveways—turning and crossing. There are a few reasons for this. The first is that it's physiologically challenging for many people to eyeball a fast-moving human-sized object in the street against chaotic, shadowy backgrounds, glare, through dirty windshields, etc. The less time a driver has to notice something the less likely it is to happen. Another reason is that many drivers tend to be psychologically unprepared for the presence of bicyclists on the street—they're subconsciously looking for cars and nothing else. Clearly the traffic code is not adequate protection for bicyclists in traffic when the greatest danger to the bicyclist is the inability of motorists to see and notice them whether they are riding lawfully or not. This very common form of motorist mistake is known as the "looked-but-failed-to-see error." Tens of thousands of lawful bicyclists are injured this way every year in this country.[24]

As a bicyclist, then, the primary task is not to plug oneself into a shaky system, but to withhold trust in it on a fundamental level. In traffic we find the very essence of fallibility. Its most important feature, if not its most prominent, is the basic human mistake. Traffic is humans and mistakes are the human condition. That's not to say bicyclists should shun the rules of the road, mind you. They just have to be realistic about them. The task is to ride always with the understanding that you could be overlooked easily by this or that mistake-prone motorist and to remember the potentially very serious consequences, and ride accordingly, rules or not.

For adult bicyclists, rule-following and safety are really two separate issues and, for safety's sake, should be recognized as such. Bicyclist lawfulness has more to do with public relations than safety. That's not to say these public relations issues aren't important. Experienced riders will read this and understand what I'm saying—the lesson will be absorbed eventually. Others will think I'm off the deep end.

The Code of Movement

Every member of any body of wheelmen would only be too glad to see the reckless riding indulged in by a certain class of riders suppressed.

Isaac Potter, 1893[25]

The attempt by a relative few latter-day Potters to contain the raucousness of the bicycle is an ongoing, massively doomed effort. A quick glance around the city reveals that bicyclists feel as unconstrained by the traffic code today as they did in the spring of 1893.

However, are the bicyclists really unique in this regard? Most everyone moving through the city seems to adhere to an unwritten Code of Movement that is based on a common-sense notion of right-of-way. This notion, indeed, has been enshrined in traffic codes since ancient times. Even though the modern traffic code contains all varieties of controls to keep people in check, in the city centers people tend to disregard any superfluous direction and default to the underlying universal code—a sort of convention of primitive courtesy. Some are better at following the Code than others, and some just ignore all laws, unwritten or otherwise. (In the parlance of the street, these people are jackholes.)

Under the Code of Movement, pedestrians may jaywalk, as long as they do it in such a way that does not disturb the commonsense rights-of-way of drivers or bicyclists in the street. And jaywalk they do. Similarly, drivers fudge their stops, speed up in response to yellow lights, and when the road finally opens up, drive five miles per hour over the speed limit. Even though cars are potentially deadly to nearby road users, citizens, even police, tolerate this behavior as long as rights-of-way aren't egregiously violated. Look around—it's not the written law that people are following. People are observed following the law, staying within their lanes and obeying traffic signals, *unless* it is convenient and relatively unobtrusive for them to do otherwise. For the most part this system, if it can be called that, serves its purpose and people get where they want to go.

In the city centers bicycles combine the speed of motor traffic with the maneuverability of pedestrians. Thus, in the wrong hands, a bicycle can make a special mess of things. On the other hand, an operator who has good awareness of his or her surroundings and is considerate can take advantage of the bicycle's special attributes in a sustainable and safe fashion. Having well figured this out, bicyclists in city centers tend to fudge the written rules in various ways. They may ride on sidewalks, which is usually illegal, or treat red lights like stop signs. The truth is that it's *possible* to do these things without ever violating the underlying right-of-way of any other pedestrian or road user, although it takes some subtle skills. One can ride a bicycle in what is technically a scofflaw fashion while remaining true to the Code of Movement, thus upsetting nobody but the stiffest of the law-and-order set, who are out of place in the cities anyway. It is also possible to do these things while blasting the Code of Movement as well as the law to pieces and leaving a trail of psychological destruction in your zigzaggy tracks, and this, more and more, is how it's done.

Law and Order

There are plenty of strict legalists out there, some bicyclists and some not—the Just-Say-Noers—who insist on bicyclists' adherence to all traffic laws, end of discussion. Their position is logical but it's proven to be unrealistic. All the logic, laws, crackdowns, and scowling—it's all failed: Bicyclists flow like water through the streets, everywhere. It's the nature of the beast. But now that bicycling is on the rise across the nation and there are noticeably more illogical riders on the streets, calls for stricter enforcement of existing laws grow louder.

Municipalities are confused, and their general outlooks on bicycling vary widely. Some feel that promoting bicycling is a fiscal imperative; others are inclined to push bicyclists off the streets entirely. Most want to encourage and crack down at the same time. What they all have in common is they want to do the right thing, don't want to spend any money doing it, and don't know what the right thing is.

We seem to be at an important point in the evolution of the country's law-enforcement stance on bicycling, a crossroads. Some agencies are leaning toward reining in the bicyclists; others decide to give 'em more rope. The legislators of Idaho finally fulfilled a long-standing fantasy of some bike advocates—they made it legal for the state's bicyclists to treat red lights like stop signs and stop signs like yield signs. Of course, most Idaho bicyclists had already been doing that, but it was nonetheless a significant moment for the bicycle in public policy, an interesting twist after the 120-year legacy of Isaac Potter's "Liberty Law." Momentum for similar liberalization was growing in San Francisco and Denver. Meanwhile, the city of Chicago, where bicyclists weren't any more shy about taking some liberties than those in other cities, was going the opposite direction, opting for a Just-Say-No crackdown against lawbreaking bikers. It wasn't the first time that officials in Chicago announced such a crackdown.[26]

The latter-day Potters spend a great deal of energy promoting "equal rights for bicyclists." These advocates maintain that it's critical for bicyclists and drivers to adhere to the very same laws, and critical for the police to ticket and harass lawbreaking riders. In this way the upstanding bicyclists who remain will finally gain the respect of everybody else and secure their freedom to use the street in a vehicular fashion. One reason these guys sound like they're talking about some parallel universe is the fact that, in many places in the United States, bicyclists have long enjoyed superior freedoms compared to their auto-driving colleagues. Bicyclists have access to much of the pedestrian realm and almost all of the vehicular realm. They have the streets, the alleys, sometimes the sidewalks, the plazas and parking lots, and even their own specially created off-street routes. Then, out in traffic, they can get away with things that drivers and motorcyclists only dream about—the equality for which some advocates strive is actually a step down.

It's time for Americans to update their traffic laws, Idaho-style, to reflect the reality that already exists on the streets. Cities like Denver and Chicago, for instance, should consider allowing bicyclists to cross through downtown intersections on the pedestrian phase of their traffic signals (when motor traffic is stopped in all four directions—the so-called "Barnes Dance," named for the traffic engineer who developed it), something that about 95 percent of riders currently do anyway, provided they do it from a stop, and while ceding the right-of-way to any pedestrians. Very much like the Idaho law.

Such a change would reward discreet and sensible bicyclists with a bit more freedom, but it could also clarify exactly what the real problem is with bicyclists using the pedestrian phase of the signal—frightening or encroaching on the rights-of-way of pedestrians—and focus efforts to stop that specific problem. Conceivably, even the pedestrians would be better off.

If bicyclists are going to run lights anyway, try to make them do it in the safest and best way possible. There is a right way and a wrong way to do it. Safe and courteous or reckless and rude. I don't see much downside to enshrining in law conservative, courteous, time-tested techniques for safely negotiating red-light intersections. I'd contend that this stands to have much less ill effect than the legalization of right turns on red that occurred in many states. I don't see much upside to forcing a careful rider to wait arbitrarily at a red that he or she could just as easily roll through without encroaching on anyone, especially if the police in most cases don't feel the need to enforce the requirement to wait. I think it's okay to legalize some of the advantages that prudent bicyclists have always enjoyed. Of course, I'm biased.

VII

THE SORRY STATE OF THE
MOTORING DREAM

Energy Density

Our civilization—such as it is—rests on cheap and convenient power.

Henry Ford, 1926[1]

MAXIM WAS UNFAMILIAR WITH THE PROPERTIES OF GASOLINE when he started on his project, so he decided to perform a little test. He placed a single drop in the bottom of metal cylinder, then threw in a match. *Blamm-o!* The scorched matchstick shot out of the cylinder like a bullet.

"It was evident," says Maxim, "that there was about a thousand times more kick in a drop of gasoline than I had pictured in my wildest flights of imagination."[2] He also did not fail to note the tremendous difference in the amount of power contained within that single drop versus the amount in his bicycling legs. Maxim had just acquainted himself with the energy density of gasoline.

The incredible amount of energy packed into refined petroleum was amazing to Maxim, but it goes virtually unnoticed today. Your average motorist does not recognize or appreciate the unique properties of the fuel that enables their motoring. To say that petroleum has been taken for granted is quite an understatement.

Americans have grown to expect abundant supplies of gasoline, but not only that—it is expected to remain dirt cheap as well. Even with gas at $4 per gallon like it was in 2008, it costs just a few shiny quarters' worth of fuel to pile all your friends in the SUV and roll under the magic power of combustion a few miles to the bar, circus, pawn shop, or wherever you want to go, surrounded by a few tons of steel and plastic and blaring stereos and DVD players. This is considered outrageously expensive.

After a few generations were born into a world of seemingly boundless supplies of explosive energy, it has become difficult to imagine things any other way. But in fact, the world of abundant, nearly free fossil-fuel energy was a very special place. Not a normal place at all. We have lived in a very weird time in history. The Age of Explosions. And a short, fleeting time it was, in the grand scheme. We sucked up hundreds of millions of years worth of slow-cooked fossil fuel—concentrated solar power—and burned it up in a one-hundred-year frenzy of consumption, such that all the cheap, easy-to-get stuff of this incredible resource is pretty much gone. That was it. It's in the rearview mirror now. It's impressive how fast we burned through the world's cheap oil. Our consumption was as concentrated as the fuel.

There will still be energy, of course, after the era of cheap oil, but it will be a different sort of energy. It'll be boutique energy. There is even a lot of oil left—it will never run out, in fact—but what's left and recoverable will take a lot more energy to extract. Consider—our oil fix is now supplied in part by reservoirs that lie nine thousand feet under water, and a further thirty thousand feet or so below the ocean floor. Imagine the tremendous amount of energy it must take to pump that crude upward over seven miles and then across the Gulf of Mexico 150 miles to the refinery. It's a far cry from the gushers of the 1930s that blew out the tops of the Texas rigs and rained black gold all over James Dean.

The alternatives that we've been starting to work up, the various candidates to replace oil, can't possibly give us nearly as much bang for the buck as the old standby. They won't have nearly as much pop. Their energy density pales in comparison. This means we simply won't be able to go as far or as fast or as cheap. For a long time we'll be going back to the same dark well to get our fix, and paying increasing amounts for the magic elixir. Oil will be taken for granted no more.

So look back on your time on this planet, in this country of all countries, in the era of cheap energy, and just smile and sigh. Those were some crazy times, eh? Energy expert Cutler Cleveland claims, "The changes wrought by fossil fuels exceeded even those produced by the introduction of fire."[3] Try to appreciate your luck in having lived in this era with all the incredible advances in civilization that rode on its coattails. Americans enjoyed decades of prosperity and security and a standard of living that was unprecedented in history. Here's hoping you got your fill.

Double Down

How the mighty have fallen!

Samuel 1:19

As the economic crisis unfolded in September 2008, something else was going on at the same time and providing what could be a disquieting glimpse into the future.

Two major hurricanes, Gustav and Ike, chugged into the Gulf and slammed into the coasts of Louisiana and Texas and the oil platforms, pipelines, and refineries there. The infrastructure weathered the storms, generally speaking, but the power grid was heavily damaged. Dozens of refineries along the coast sat lifeless for weeks as crews scrambled to restore electricity to the plants. About 3.5 million barrels per day worth of gasoline ceased flowing eastbound in the Colonial pipeline and the associated pipes that supply all the Southeast states. That's a lot of missing fuel, more than one-third of the country's daily gasoline consumption.

The nation's gasoline stocks were already dipping below the normal range before the hurricanes hit, so analysts predicted well in advance that the storms would result in rather pronounced shortages in areas supplied by the Texas refineries. When the pipes started to dry up, officials in these affected areas seemed committed to a policy of denial of the existence of shortages and warning retailers against "price gouging"—a crime with various subjective definitions. Beyond the usual pandering, officials were in a tough spot here. Even though they knew shortages were likely, they also knew that announcing that fact would cause people to freak out and start hoarding, potentially making the problem worse. When the shortages became evident to the wider population—despite the disingenuous assurances from on high—that is indeed what happened. Drivers in Nashville, Atlanta, Tallahassee, Charlotte, and Asheville lost it a bit when some of the pumps started to run dry. Instead of careful stewardship to ensure adequate supplies for essential uses of this suddenly scarce resource, precisely the opposite occurred. Drivers met increasing shortages with increasing desperation and selfishness. They waited in long lines to top off their tanks and the five-gallon tank in the trunk. They cut into forty-car lines and got into fistfights. They drove all around their cities, wasting gas, looking for gas, and left the lifeless hulks of their vehicles by the roadsides when the tanks finally went dry. Drivers began to arrive at stations before dawn in some locations, hoping to catch the next shipment. They were disrupting their lives in extreme predawn ways in hopes of avoiding disruptions caused by the gas shortage. Looking for someone to blame, they threatened the various governors who, remember, had assured them that plenty of fuel would be available. Atlanta drivers called for the impeachment of Georgia Governor Sonny Perdue and appeared on the verge of going all Lord of the Flies as the shortage persisted and worsened.

In short, drivers treated the shortage like a true emergency. This is no exaggeration, according to 911 dispatchers in the greater Atlanta area. Their phone systems were clogged by drivers seeking locations of stations with gas for sale.[4] The situation revealed a citizenry emotionally dependent on their cars. Some Atlanta residents decided that they were unable to get to work because they couldn't find gasoline. These drivers who suddenly lost use of their legs managed never to notice that others in these same communities had been getting to work on time and traveling around their whole adult lives without ever having owned cars of their own. Unfortunately, the unreasonable panic of the pampered, able-bodied drivers in these communities did in fact create true emergencies for some who really do rely on their vehicles, for instance, elderly or disabled folks and various types of tradesmen.

Eventually those in charge were forced to acknowledge that the fuel shortages were real and would last for a while, and very gingerly, they started making suggestions to the folks at home on different ways to cope with the situation. You might try carpooling, working from home, or using MARTA, whispered officials in Atlanta. Asheville Mayor Terry Bellamy echoed these suggestions and urged drivers involved in desperate quests for gas to call around to different stations (not 911) instead of driving around randomly.[5] They can tell people to take the train, take the day off, or carpool. They can even tell people to take the bus. However, there is one thing they absolutely must not suggest if they value their political careers. You cannot remind people that they might be able to ride a bike, or in any way move under their own power. Clearly, mere mention of these options is viewed as political suicide and is studiously avoided. The people are angry enough as it is! In that tense environment mouthing the word "bicycle" might cause a mob with pitchforks to descend on the state capitol, if only the mob could find gas. Pitchfork-wielding mobs don't walk anymore; they arrive in SUVs.

None of this bodes well for the future. The situation did provide a teaching moment for the nation, though. Ahead of the next impending shortages it's likely we will see politicians a little more proactive. It's quite possible that some form of rationing will be applied and it's more likely these measures will be politically acceptable. Rationing schemes have already been worked out by government bureaucrats who've had several decades to think about it. If we get more of these abrupt supply disruptions in the future, expect the authorities to distribute gasoline vouchers to registered car owners. If that happens, car owners who are willing to move under their own power might be able to make a tidy profit selling their vouchers to less willful individuals. The Department of Energy's Standby Gasoline Rationing Plan states, "A white market will be permitted for the sale of transfer of ration rights."[6] But no price gouging, people.

Depletion Never Rests

Many still seem to subscribe to what has been derisively labeled the "cornucopian" view of oil production. That is, if we need it, we'll find it. In this view, plenty of oil is there for the taking, and oil companies will extract it as long as it's economically sensible for them to do so, never you worry. People who agree with this line of thinking will often cite fantastic numbers for global oil reserves, and rarely mention any technical, practical, or on-the-ground issues—shortage of functioning drilling rigs, for instance—that might limit the rate of extraction of said reserves. To the cornucopian, the enterprise of oil extraction is not unlike an electronic transfer of funds. Those who envision oil being conjured instantaneously from the depths by its own demand from a virtually unlimited reservoir will obviously not see any legitimate supply issues on the horizon. Spikes in price must then be pinned on any one or combination of myriad other factors—the manipulations of OPEC, the speculators, the oilmen in the White House.* Oil is seen as rightfully cheap and any price spike a deviation that will be corrected with a stern whuppin' when Daddy Market gets home. The upshot is the economy keeps growing as far as the eye can see, unrestrained by energy supply issues. "We don't know where this abundance will come from . . . we just know that it will appear," wrote Shawn Tully, an editor at *Fortune*, succinctly explaining the cornucopian philosophy.[7]

Tully and others might have felt pretty smug in the fall of 2008 after the price of oil tumbled quickly to about a third of its July peak. But the drop was due to a reversal in

---

*The notion that shadowy speculators were responsible for the spike of 2007–08 was gaining a great deal of traction when the Commodities Futures Trading Commission investigated and released a report on the market in July 2008. The report concluded that the spike was not inconsistent with supply-and-demand and noted that inventories had declined. Just a few weeks later, however, the CFTC disclosed that a single trading outfit controlled no less than 11 percent of all the oil contracts traded on the New York Mercantile Exchange for July. The CFTC did not reveal the name of the firm but a subsequent *Washington Post* report named the Swiss firm Vitol as the culprit.[8]

the economy, from growth to contraction, which turned oil demand on its heels. This is Big Daddy Market at work, but not in the way Tully projected. Tully's main assertion/assumption—that ample new deposits of oil will be discovered and developed to power an eventual resumption of global economic growth and ever-increasing demand—remains to be seen. Those mythical deposits just aren't being discovered. At present, and perhaps for years to come, they aren't needed, but when the world starts rocking and rolling again, it might find itself bumping up against a glass ceiling set by the same lack of new supply that existed when the economy tanked.

To put it mildly, the cornucopians are missing a great deal with their ideological semi-analysis. For instance, an appreciation of the many ways reality can intrude on flow rate. (For example, the vast majority of oil is controlled by nations, not oil companies, and its production depends as much on politics as economics.) More important, the reality of the ongoing, perhaps accelerating, declines in production from many of the world's most prolific oil fields seems to have escaped the cornucopians entirely. Depletion of the world's giant oil fields is the plot twist upon which this tale turns. About half of the world's oil fix is supplied by the largest 2 percent of fields—that's just over one hundred fields, out of more than four thousand worldwide.[9] A few things are critical to understand about these giant fields. First of all, very few of them have been discovered within the past few decades. And many of the most productive oil fields in history are in precipitous, irreversible decline. An early peak followed by a steep, irreversible decline is the norm for any oil field's production profile.

The huge fields in Texas made the United States the top oil producer in the world for quite a while and gave Americans the comforting sensation of sitting atop a virtually free source of energy that would never run out. Abundance. Production from these fields was held at a low boil for many years by production limits meant to keep the domestic industry from drowning in its own good fortune.[10] The limits were removed in 1969, when nationalization of Saudi oil appeared imminent and various other writings were observed on the wall, and large quantities of fecal matter could be seen hurtling toward a very giant fan. Quite soon after the spigots were opened in Texas, those fields peaked. And they've been on the descent ever since, mirroring the bigger picture of all domestic production (which topped out in 1970 at around 10.5 million barrels per day). Despite pulling out all the stops with creative drilling and exploration and high-tech extraction methods, current production from Texas is a mere puddle compared to the ocean we wallowed in during the Age of Aquarius.

Oil from Prudhoe Bay, Alaska came on line at exactly the right time in the mid-1970s, after America had been dangled over the cliff by its new oil overlords and had lost its cool as well as its control over energy. Prudhoe Bay was a huge producer, a so-called supergiant, that changed the global oil game and once again stroked America gently on the head, slipped it a roofie, and put it to sleep with happy thoughts of oil abundance and security. Prudhoe ramped up quickly and plateaued for almost ten years at about 1.5 million barrels per day. Then, around 1988, the plateau crumbled. Twenty years beyond its glory days, Prudhoe spits out approximately 20 percent of what it once did, and output continues to diminish. We'll squeeze that sucker for decades to come, and it will continue to be an important source, but it will only produce a fraction of the volume that flowed at peak.

The *deus ex machina* of Prudhoe Bay felt good while it lasted. Now, however, the missing 1.2 million barrels per day to which America grew accustomed must come from somewhere else. Depletion—this is how Americans become more dependent on foreign sources of energy with each passing day. Prudhoe Bay was a soothing bedtime story, but now the nation comes to after a three-decade blackout, with a headache and a vague sensation of having done many embarrassing things.

Oil in the North Sea was also found and extracted with lovely timing. Here was another huge supply of precious non-OPEC oil suddenly appearing on the scene at what seemed to be a very opportune time for global capitalism. The great fields off the shores of Norway and England were tapped into during the 1970s, showcases for the latest high-tech extraction methods. Then, lickety-split, the fields peaked in the 1980s. The United Kingdom's famous Forties field currently produces around 10 percent of its peak volume; the Brent field is also crapping out. The Norwegian giants Ekofisk, Oseberg, and Gullfaks are all down to about 20 percent of their peak levels. The era of great volumes of energy flowing from beneath the North Sea is fading. Russia, second only to Saudi Arabia among oil producers, is also struggling to maintain production levels against a backdrop of depletion of its star fields. Its supergiant Samotlor, for instance, has sunk from over three million barrels per day to about three hundred thousand.[11] The collapse in oil prices was crushing their fragile economy late in 2008.

In August 2008 the Mexican state oil company Pemex reported that its flagship field, Cantarell, the largest and most important in the Western Hemisphere, was declining at an astonishing rate of 36 percent per year.[12] The Mexican oil dilemma, which becomes the American oil dilemma, is the global dilemma on a national scale. The depletion of Mexico's largest, most productive field could not be offset by gains elsewhere in the country. Pemex cannot find and exploit new sources of petroleum as fast as the stuff from *el grande* Cantarell is going away. The end result is that Mexico exports an ever decreasing amount of oil to the United States, which depends on those exports. At this rate Mexico will be consuming all of its own production within a few years and will turn from exporter to importer, with far-reaching implications.

Doing the math of global oil depletion is not exactly soothing. With so many important fields in accelerating decline, the difference has to be made up with large numbers of far less productive, more expensive sources. Global oil production goes one step forward and two steps back. The giant fields produce huge numbers, then the magnitude of the emptiness left behind when they decline is correspondingly huge. As the giants tumble down the back sides of their production curves, it is estimated by the Energy Information Administration's conservative model that oil producers have to add 4.4 million barrels to daily supply every year just to keep up with declines from existing fields. In ten years we will need to have found 44 million barrels of daily production that we don't have today. That's more than half of global consumption and more than twice as much as we currently use in this country. Just to stay even. It's enough to make a cornucopian cry, but I'll settle for some second thoughts.

Pie in the Ground

Oil versus water. Which do you like better? We may have to remind ourselves before too long.

On the Western Slope of the Colorado Rockies, in a land of buttes where the desert transitions to mountains, sits a huge geologic formation called Green River. The Green River formation is composed of all the tiny dead beasts and leafy plants that were left over from the millions of years this area was covered with a shallow sea. Combined with rain the Green River shale becomes a molasses-like glop that stops cars and bicycles in their tracks. It would have become oil eventually, if it had been buried deep enough in the earth and cooked for, say, a few hundred million years. But calling the Green River formation "oil shale" is a misnomer; the most the formation can offer is keragen, which can only be transformed into an "oil-like substance"—oil junior—by cooking it for a long time at about one thousand degrees. The latest scheme offered by Royal Dutch Shell to extract petroleum from the Green River formation is among the most surreal-sounding industrial proposals you are ever likely to hear from a major corporation. They propose filling the earth with hundreds of giant electrified tubes to cook the keragen in situ for three years. In cooking the keragen they hope to turn it into something more closely resembling oil, which could then be pumped out. The project would require the building of its own dedicated power plant, which would be the largest coal-fired plant in the state. The company said such an operation could eventually produce about one hundred thousand barrels per day of oil-like substance—about one half of one one-hundredth of daily consumption in the U.S., to keep this large-sounding number in perspective. Producing more than that would require more huge coal-burning power plants.

The process of conjuring petroleum from Colorado earth would thus be very energy intensive. Net energy gains (expressed as a ratio of energy return on energy invested, or EROEI), if there are any, would be a mere sliver of the amount of energy contained in the formation. Perhaps more important, the CO_2 emissions from the operation may make it a no-go in the coming era of carbon taxes and whatnot. Huge coal-burning plants may be a thing of the past in a carbon-conscious political environment.

Producing this oil will also ruin a great deal of water—about three barrels per every barrel of oil produced; in addition, the project would "contaminate local surface water with salts and toxics that leach from spent shale."[13] (There's nothing particularly special about oil shale operations' potential to consume and pollute water. Oil-versus-water is a familiar story in the oil industry. The most obvious example is the process known as hydraulic fracturing. Since the 1950s companies like Halliburton have been pumping highly pressurized water and a secret soup of chemicals into the ground around oil, coal, and natural gas deposits to open fissures in the rock and ease extraction of the goods. The environmental threats associated with the widely used process remain largely unstudied, much to the industry's delight.[14])

When it comes down to it, projects like Shell's could make heaps of money for the company while remaining a sour deal for society at large, providing very little net gain in energy at an environmental cost that overwhelms the benefits. It's too easy to jump on the oil companies for messing with the environment, for messing with our heads with their incessant propaganda, for messing with our government process with their buyoffs and lobbying. They are just doing what oil companies can be expected to do. Start worrying if they *don't* do those things. But what about us? Every drop Shell takes out of the ground, we burn it up and come slinking back for more. Demand, they call it. It's a serious-sounding word, but much of our oil consumption is frivolous. Our government officials fail to protect the public good as they are charged to do, but these are our representatives (or appointees thereof) who we elect, tolerate, and neglect to put behind bars. The problem is right in front of us, as long as we're standing in front of a mirror. Quite often the mirror is actually the side window of a tragically hip vehicle, into which we can gaze while standing at the gas pump.

The ongoing push for development of the "oil shale resource" could be the clearest proof yet of this country's irrational and self-destructive devotion to oil consumption, to dig and cook and burn oil at any cost, even if it's not oil. The drive to consume even while destroying ourselves in the process fits perfectly with the clinical definition of addiction.[15] Going after the keragen around Grand Junction would be a bit like a heroin junkie raiding a bakery for poppy seeds. It's nothing more than a cry for help.

If you could take water and turn it into oil, would you do it? The Colorado keragen crisis brings us face to face with some of the most pitiful aspects of humanity. Time to take a long hard look in the mirror.

Substitute Phrases

One sector where we've seen a clear sea change is complaining, which is its own industry now, called "Pain at the Pump." Since the phrase "Pain at the Pump" has been used so relentlessly in 2007-08 (a Google search of the exact phrase brought up about a half million hits in July 2008), it has lost a great deal of that luster it once had. It used to be quite lustrous. So I took the liberty to conjure some substitute phrases that folks might use instead of the haggard standby. Feel free to use "Nerves at the Nozzle," "Strapped at the Station," "Whining at the Well," "Sputtering at the Spout," or "Tears at the Tank." Obviously it's going to be difficult to replace such a near perfect phrase as "Pain at the Pump." We could never truly replace it. We can only hope to rest it for a while.

The holy grail is to find a phrase that starts with Angst. But that, unfortunately, has remained out of reach. We will keep drilling for it.

In the fall of 2008 a local news anchor in Hoboken attempted to use the phrase "Pain at the Pump" and the "Main Street/Wall Street" juxtaposition in quick succession while introducing a story, and her head actually exploded.

Fallacies of History, or Not

A lot of folks of a certain age may be feeling waves of déjà vu. Haven't we seen all this before? Back in the 1970s people cried about our dependence on Middle Eastern oil just as they do now. And they started making all kinds of noise about solar power and started importing tiny cars. Some people may even remember warnings from that era about an impending peak in global oil production. Is there an echo in here?

We all know what happened next. Oil didn't peak. Not even close. In fact, it got ridiculously cheap again and flowed like water. Just as we see today, demand for oil contracted after the price shocks of the 1970s—quite significantly and for many years after the 1979 crisis—but demand eventually resumed rising past what many had thought were impossible levels. It's no wonder that people are inclined to sneer at the latest warnings, which sound suspiciously like those we heard in the 1970s, minus the bell-bottoms.

The 1973 oil crisis was the product of an oil embargo by the Arab oil producers on the United States and the Netherlands* in response to these countries' support for Israel during the Arab-Israeli War of that year (the October War or Yom Kippur War). The embargo didn't last long, but it was a jolt to the economies of the United States, Europe, and Japan. With Iran still in the pocket of Uncle Sam's crazy striped pants, the United States had a little more cushion than the Europeans and Japanese. The crisis spurred fundamental changes in transportation and energy policies in Europe and Japan, while policies in the United States continued on their fundamentally different, oil-slurping course.

If we look a little closer at this crisis, we see that it occurred in the larger context of a decline in domestic oil production—which had peaked a few years earlier—and skyrocketing demand around the world. Between 1970 and 1978 global demand for oil grew from about forty-five million barrels per day to about sixty-five million barrels per day.[17] The Arab oil exporters had embargoed the West during the 1967 war as well, but that embargo had been toothless against American production capabilities at the time. By 1973 the market was much tighter and the United States was vastly more dependent on OPEC's good graces.

In 1979 Iran jumped out of Uncle Sam's coin pocket. In addition to the other well-known calamities associated with

---

*The Netherlands was singled out, not so much because of the Dutch government's policies, but rather because much of the oil supplied to northern Europe came in at the port of Rotterdam.[16]

the event, the Islamist ouster of our buddy the Shah led to the choking off of more than four million barrels per day. This was a more acute energy predicament than the crisis of '73. Oil prices launched skyward, reaching over $40 per barrel in 1980. That's something like $110 in inflation-adjusted 2008 dollars. You know the rest: gas lines, cardigans, a lengthy recession. Jimmy Carter crucified for challenging Americans' habits of energy consumption.

Those who lived through these crises couldn't help but notice that the world didn't end. The supply crunches never came to any sort of world-changing culmination, as had been promised. The country was shocked in the general direction of frugality for a period but the shock wore off eventually and we were driving bigger, thirstier vehicles and happily pouring cheap gas into those tanks without a second thought. What happened? Well, the 1973 embargo ended quickly, for one thing, the Arab oil producers sufficiently mollified. What's more, Alaska's Prudhoe oil field came on line in the mid-'70s, along with significant North Sea fields and Cantarell in Mexico, huge new producers that changed the game.

And then there was Saudi Arabia. Making up for shortfalls in crude extraction within the United States, a separate and a more serious challenge than the embargo, Saudi Arabia ramped up its operation, producing more than 8 million barrels per day by 1974, up from about 2.5 million barrels per day in 1965. As the swing producer for the world, the Kingdom was extremely compliant with American wishes for decades. During the energy crisis of 1979-80 and then again a decade later, when Iraq's invasion of Kuwait and the subsequent Gulf War slashed global oil production by more than five million barrels per day, the Saudis responded by opening their wells full blast to stabilize world markets and keep the price in check. After the Iranian Revolution they let fly with a blast of ten million barrels per day for a time; during the Gulf War they opened the floodgates again, quickly raising their production by three million barrels per day. The Saudis' ability and willingness to generate these monumental increases led people to believe that such ability and willingness would always be there.[18]

In short, the full flow of oil resumed and continued to increase after '73 and '79. If the current energy mess is like the previous ones, it will fizzle into a period of hyperabundance that will collapse the price of oil—so far so good. It must also lead into a resumption of growth far past previous levels of consumption whenever the springtime of the economy comes around again. In truth, nobody knows for sure what will happen, but considering that producers' struggle just to keep up with ongoing depletion of their aging oil fields, the possibility of growing the rate of global production significantly above the eighty-six-million-barrel-per-day plateau becomes more and more remote. The prospect of rising above and beyond the 100 million-barrel-per-day mark, as predicted by the International Energy Agency, seems like a crazy fantasy. It's not just the longhaired freaks who see things that way. ConocoPhillips CEO James Mulva said in 2007: "I don't think we are going to see the supply going over 100 million barrels a day and the reason is, where is all that oil going to come from?"[19]

Maybe we should be thinking of these oil upheavals in a fundamentally different way. Instead of a series of separate crises, they could very well be part of one large-scale crisis. Not a new idea, of course. The big-C Crisis can then be traced at least as far back as 1970, when domestic oil production peaked. Perhaps the Crisis could be traced even to the 1950s, when we first surpassed our ability to satisfy our energy thirst with homegrown supply. From that point onward we were living beyond our means. The roots of our present floundering reach back at least half a century.

What Happened in Europe

The cure is not to reduce the price, but, on the contrary, to raise it even higher to break our addiction to oil.

Anders Fogh Rasmussen, Danish Prime Minister, 2008[20]

Drivers in Europe have been paying the equivalent of $8 to $10 per gallon, and as such, they watched our panic over $4 gas with a combination of amusement and the usual annoyance. *Silly Ameri-cahns!*

Things are different in Europe, you may have noticed. Trains, hedgerows, neon-colored backpacks. Fundamental differences in the transportation sector. It varies a great deal from country to country and city to city, but the Euros tend to cycle commute and bike for transportation purposes on the order of ten to twenty times as much as Americans, or more. Copenhagen is said to sport an astounding 50 percent bicycling mode share. Why? Several reasons. The European cities have suburbs but the workforce tends to live close to their jobs. The cities have been engineered with dedicated cycle path networks that effectively service commuter traffic. And gas is much more expensive there. Gas is more expensive in Europe because the European nations made it so. Unblessed with the kind of oil reserves we blew through in the United States and recognizing their particular vulnerability during the crisis of the early 1970s, the Europeans raised taxes on fuel high enough to spur fundamental shifts in the way their societies operate. When the North Sea oil bonanza came on line, they were able to completely eliminate their need to import oil from the Middle East. The Russians still have them by the short-n-curlies with regard to natural gas.

The European attitude toward transportational bicycling turns out to be a bit like the European attitude toward sex. Compared to Americans, they are not nearly as freaked out by such things. They're not going to start jabbering like Beavis if they see a bare breast; if they see a guy on a bike, they're not going to pull up next to him and scream, "Yeeeaaaaarrggh Lance!" They give the impression of having been there before.

There is much to recommend in the European approach to bicycling and transportation, but American bicycling advocates should be careful about calls to follow directly along in Europe's cycle paths. This is something that American bicycle advocates often dream about, turning American cities into

Amsterdam, with dedicated cycle tracks everywhere and high-cheekboned people transporting themselves deliberately along on three-speeds. Considering current fiscal constraints, applying the vision here is a highly unrealistic proposition, and that may be just as well.

Some of the path systems in European cities are absolutely amazing. Americans would be astounded to see what the Dutch, Danes, Finns, Norwegians, and Germans have created for bicycle transportation. I like much of what they've done there, but in the end, call me crazy, I'm not convinced their path systems represent the best possible infrastructure setup for bicyclists. Maybe my brain is addled after so many years on the streets. But I like the streets. I like the American streets, the dance of traffic, the occasional flashes of terror and drafting off ambulances. The Amsterdam cycle path paradigm is nice in different ways, but it's kind of a plodding enterprise. Kind of slow and clogged up, confining. We bicyclists in America are surely in more danger than our Euro counterparts, perhaps less accepted in the national culture, but we may also have a little more freedom overall. We can ride with a little more speed, a little more zing. The trade-off goes largely unappreciated.

American transportational bicyclists should relish and cultivate and enjoy their place on the streets, in my opinion. There isn't much alternative for us at this point, nor would there appear to be one on the horizon, considering the ongoing fiscal implosions and national devotion to a future of driving. It's possible that bicycle infrastructure will get a significant boost from a new presidential administration engulfed in stimulus mania, but there is almost no chance that any American city, even the most bike-crazy, would be able to create the type of comprehensive cycle path system that is enjoyed by the commuters of northern Europe. Instead, it would seem to me, our Euro envy is much more likely to spawn half-measures and dead-end ideas. We'll get a few Euro-style cycle paths or separated bike lanes next to streets that bicyclists have been safely riding upon for over a hundred years. We'll get token projects that look good for politicians and make people feel fuzzy inside and fail to improve overall conditions for bicyclists.

The best system, I believe, would be one that maintains and enhances the bicyclists' right to ride the streets, in the mix with the cars, but also features a sprinkling of effective bike paths that pass beneath the street grid along with rivers, canals, and rail corridors. These paths are the most coveted form of infrastructure as they allow bicyclists to traverse significant cross-town distances without encountering any stop signs, red lights, or street intersections. A system like that would represent the best from both sides of the Atlantic. Why not?

Such a hybrid system is not all that different than those already in place in Minneapolis, San Francisco, and Denver. These cities and a scattering of others are on the right track. In other towns that have very little bike-related infrastructure, installing and maintaining a few highly useful, fully separated paths and slapping down a bunch of large and properly placed sharrows constitutes a workable, relatively affordable strategy to promote bicycle transportation. It won't make a perfect world but it will have a significant positive impact. Thinking we can steadily transform Portland into Oulu is nothing but a trap.

The American way of bicycling does not need to be fundamentally changed, it only needs to be enhanced. We in the States could actually do Europe one better in our bicycling future. We could ride farther, and faster, on sportier bicycles, and just generally have more fun with it. *Silly Ameri-cahns.*

New Visions

Would it be surprising if thousands of Americans were this very day sitting in downtown gridlock, sucking fumes, watching the gas gauge drop, and experiencing Maxim-style mental upheavals concerning their current mode of travel? Anybody having a vision out there? Traffic congestion has matured right along with vehicle performance, widening the chasm between the Dream and reality, intensifying the dissatisfaction and frustration of those behind the wheel. Drivers become sitters. Instead of looking down at their cranks and bemoaning the human engine, as Maxim did between Salem and Lynn, might they be looking around at their spacious yet stationary cars and trucks and trying to imagine something that could somehow keep moving, trying to retrieve an image from the deepest folds of the brain of some sort of vehicle skinny enough to navigate through and around all this clogged traffic?

Through the twin stepmothers of congestion and control—licensing, insurance, rules, signals, lanes, speed traps, etc.—our motorized steeds have been broken, hamstrung. Much of the adventure and excitement of motoring has been sucked out, leaving, primarily, memories and ad copy. The freedom of motoring, 'twas a worthy dream but it never stood a chance. There were too many people out there, but not enough room to accommodate them in their space-hogging private cars—a simple losing equation. The motorcar became … pedestrian. The car isn't even moving a lot of the time, and there's no adventure in that. In a vehicle that wants to move but can't, DVD players, navigation devices, and other distracting doodads become necessities. The proliferation of video screens inside motor vehicles increases directly in proportion to the coefficient of immovable, stacked traffic. Even the motorcyclist (riding anywhere but California, where lane-splitting is de facto allowed) will be sitting there along with the cars, foot on the pavement, with little time left over for fulfilling the Wild Bunch legacy.

And so, in a stark turnaround, the bicycle again becomes the machine of choice for adventurers. The problem for the adventurers is that most of them don't realize it.

Of course, not everybody wants adventure. Some people may be looking for as little adventure as possible, and these folks will go right on sitting in their cars, numbed a bit by carbon monoxide and marking their place in the universe by the taillights ahead, until death comes or the price of gas drives them insane. But anyone hoping for some adventure in their transportation through the congested urban environment—a noble desire, I declare—will have to find it with some other type of vehicle. If they can imagine such a thing.

Bonfire of the Vanities

Political columnist Robert Novak is one in whom this noble desire for adventure while commuting has been notoriously strong. A self-described frustrated race car driver (not unlike this author), Novak loved the thrill of driving fast and furious in his black late-model Corvette. Unfortunately, he didn't get to experience that thrill very often, as traffic conditions along his normal routes in metro D.C., not to mention various strategically placed law enforcement officers, combined to prevent much Parnelli Jones–style driving. This apparently left him frustrated, as he was observed yelling at people out the window of his car on the streets of the nation's capital.

On July 23, 2008, Novak hit a pedestrian while driving to work. The pedestrian was crossing with the green light when Novak's car struck him during a right on red. The victim was tossed up onto the 'Vette's hood and windshield and rolled off, according to a witness. Novak kept going. A bike commuter named David Bono (the aforementioned witness) chased Novak down, which wasn't difficult as the Corvette quickly became blocked behind a wall of D.C. traffic. Bono put himself and his bike in front of Novak's car to prevent the columnist from taking off, which Bono claimed he was trying to do the whole time. Eventually Novak pulled over to wait for police, and later he emerged from a police cruiser with a single $50 ticket for failure to yield.[21] The eight-six-year-old victim suffered a dislocated shoulder but was cheered by the news of the identity of the driver who ran him down.

A few hundred quite similar car-pedestrian collisions are written up in police reports around the country every day; for 2008 we can expect a total of sixty or seventy thousand, including about forty-five hundred fatalities. Approximately one in five drivers involved in these wrecks will hit-and-run.[22]

Novak had established himself as one of the most despised journalists in Washington when this occurred, having earned the nickname "Prince of Darkness" long before he was vilified for outing CIA operative Valerie Plame in 2003.[23] The blogosphere leapt into a Novak-bashing spree—not only did the columnist appear to hit-and-run, but it looked like he was going to get away with it as well. The whole thing seemed pregnant with symbolism. Jeers and catcalls poured in from all sides.

For his part, Novak says that he never saw the guy or felt the impact, and blamed this on a grave medical condition. Indeed, less than a week after the event he was diagnosed with a large and malignant brain tumor and was told that he had six months to a year to live. Such a condition certainly could alter cognitive function and hinder the ability to perform tasks like driving a Corvette with the requisite zest while noticing pedestrians. So I think he deserves some benefit of the doubt on this one, even if several witnesses expressed dismay that anyone could fail to notice such a solid, loud impact.[24]

But what I really want to direct your attention to here, something you probably missed at first glance, is the way someone on a bicycle can carve through traffic in a crowded city, and the way someone in a car can't, no matter how badly they want to. Aggressive driver in black Corvette, strapped to four hundred horses, stuck. Easily nabbed by citizen cycle commuter, traveling under own power. This wasn't some messenger or alley-cat racer, carving traffic like a madman; this was just another bike commuter, a lawyer headed to the office. We could substitute Novak with Dale Junior and David Bono with an old lady on a three-speed with a basket in front, and the result would be about the same. Such is the sorry state of the motoring dream.

The White Van Episode

The Novak drama reminded me a bit of another I witnessed a few years back, one that shows the bicyclist's vulnerability alongside its supreme mobility. I was unlocking my bike in downtown Denver and glanced up just in time to watch a white van ram into a bicyclist who was riding plainly in sight in the right-most through lane of a busy street, directly in front of said van. There's that vulnerability I was talking about. It looked like the van driver was trying to change lanes to get around the bike and misjudged the vectors—either that or he hit the guy on purpose and took off. The bike's rear wheel crumpled and the rider fell entangled in the machine, cutting his leg a bit on the chainring. As it turns out, I knew this fellow who was scurrying off the street with his broken bike. Seeing that my friend was more or less all right, I took off after the van. It was easy to find, stopped at a red light about five blocks away. Eyes flickered nervously in the rearview mirror. On a bicycle I poked through five blocks of clogged traffic unceremoniously and rolled directly to this guy's side window, where I (ever so gently, of course) compelled him to return to the scene. He claimed not to have noticed the collision, but then, any hit-and-runner caught with their pants that far down would have to say that.

The bicycle is uniquely suited for chasing down hit-and-runners in the urban core. You don't often hear that in the sales pitch, but there it is.

New Demands

The tremendous amount of capital invested in the manufacture of cars, tires, accessories … the vast army of labor engaged directly or indirectly in the making and distributing of machines … If this is all wasted capital and extravagance then there is something seriously lacking with the American public.

C. W. Matheson, owner of Matheson Automobile
Company, 1910, a few years before
the company went bankrupt.[25]

Most drivers in this country do not feel sufficiently put-upon by current levels of traffic congestion to reach for modes that aren't as affected by it. They'd rather continue driving, even if it means sitting in traffic jams for substantial blocks of time every day.

People do respond to the price of fuel, however. Observers were dazzled this past summer by an abrupt about-face—the first drop in oil consumption in the United States in twenty years.[26] Oil consumption in the United States had been climbing steadily with a few minor hitches in its giddyup for more than a century, so a clear turnaround at the dawn of a new era in energy, at the dawn of a major recession, had the feel of a turning point of historic proportions. Could that have been Peak Domestic Gasoline Demand right there? Not everybody is ready to think about Peak Demand, so be careful. Contained within the idea of Peak Demand is the end of traditional concepts of economic growth, and thus the end of American capitalism as we know and understand it.

Whether it was the $4 gas or the recession or both or the chicken or the egg, Americans were jolted into changing their habits in 2008. Analysts continued to track domestic oil consumption obsessively, but the number wasn't as important as it used to be. The United States used to be the swing demander. While our degree of thirst for oil used to drive the market, it may now be too late for American consumers to have a decisive effect. This is a rather ironic development for the country that consumes vastly more oil per capita than any other country. Americans are far and away the world-champion consumers. Due to the gigantic populations of China and India, however, these countries have become the new drivers of world oil demand. Running into 2008, "Chindia" was generating double-digit growth in energy consumption. In India most of the vehicles run on diesel, and demand for diesel there had been growing at a ridiculous rate. The *Times of India* reported in August 2008 that demand for diesel in the region of Chennai had grown 35 percent over the previous year and that officials in that city were registering four hundred to five hundred new vehicles every day. The number was dwarfed by the number being registered in Mumbai.[27]

Twenty years ago there were virtually no privately owned cars in China and the few drivers there were required by law to keep their headlights off at night, to keep from blinding all the bicyclists.[28] In 2007 General Motors sold over three hundred thousand Buicks in China—twice as many as they sold in the United States. There are now sixteen million or so privately owned cars in China, and they are all required to keep their lights on at night. While it's growing fast, the current crop of cars in China is still extremely small compared to what's possible in a country of 1.3 billion people. Compare that to the United States, where there are more privately owned cars than registered drivers. The motorization of China can then be seen as a snowball just beginning its roll down a fourteen-thousand-foot peak.[29]

But will this snowball run out of snow, that is the question. Analysts who thought, or hoped, the emerging markets were "decoupled" from the Western economies found their assumptions flattened in 2008, along with Chindia's growth. That slowdown might have been fortuitous, as all of this Chindia frenzy points to potential big problems for the earth's future. More precisely, problems for the earth's inhabitants' future. The big picture, frankly, is alarming. Consider the vast inequalities in oil consumption that are currently observed around the globe. The average Japanese consumed fourteen barrels of oil in 2007; the average Euro consumed seventeen. Along comes the average American, belly hanging out a bit, Hawaiian shirt. The average American used twenty-five barrels in 2007, almost twice as much as the average Japanese citizen.[30]

Now check out the current per-capita consumption in China. It's comparatively minuscule, not even on the scale with the rich countries. But now they too want a seat at the banquet and their consumption promises to skyrocket accordingly. Put aside for a moment the mystery of how this additional petroleum will be produced or secured. If the Chinese and Indians begin to consume petroleum at even a modest per-capita rate, say a rate approaching that of the comparatively frugal Japanese, it is difficult to imagine how the living beings of Earth could survive the resulting ecological calamity. But the Chinese and Indians don't want to burn gas like the Japanese, oh no. They want to burn gas American-style. They feel it is their right to do so.

Why don't you go over there and tell them this: "Even though we here in America consumed energy far in excess of our reasonable needs for so long—well, more like *because* we here in America consumed energy far in excess of our reasonable needs for so long—there is not enough global ecological leeway left for any other country to do the same. We used up all the leeway. Sorry, guys. We regret to inform you that the party is over." And then run away really fast.

Child Drivers

Even people who enjoy bicycling very much may yearn on occasion to be ushered along via motor, with no more physical effort than twisting a throttle or playing footsie with a gas pedal. Count me among them. Driving a motor vehicle is like a child's dream come true. And that's a big part of the problem.

In the interest of full disclosure, the author has done some things behind the wheel that would make Barney Oldfield himself spit up. As a child driver he impaled a '73 Volkswagen Type III on a hydrant while playing four-wheel drift on a snowy night. "Radioactive" by the Firm was on the radio. There was a complex incident involving a '74 Impala—no more solid battleship ever launched from Detroit than this beauty—going backward through a fence at high speed, shearing off four-by-fours as if they were matchsticks. It would take a page or two to explain the obtuse angles and multifaceted maneuvers involved in that mishap, which still elude even partial understanding by individuals who happened to be inside the vehicle, and others who were hanging partially out of it.

Kids have a disease that prevents them from comprehending the potentially horrific consequences of their actions while driving, while doing anything, until it's too late. Until they actually feel it for themselves. In my case I had plenty of clues. Of course, like every other kid, I ignored them. I clearly remember standing on the front lawn talking to a friend one night. I must have been about fourteen or fifteen years old, no doubt chomping at the bit for the day when I could drive legally. Mid-1980s. It was a nice quiet summer night. About a mile away from the house, there was a road that went down a long, steep hill. We could hear a car hauling down the hill, its big engine roaring, faster and faster. I never saw the car or heard what kind it was, but to this day I imagine, unrealistically, a '57 Chevy. My friend and I paused in our conversation to listen to this thing blasting down the hill. Then we heard a loud crash. And another, and another, and another. We knew then exactly what we had heard—the car flipping through the air and hitting the ground repeatedly at high speed. Then we listened to all the sirens converging on the spot. The next day we read that all the kids in the car were dead at the scene. Not only that, but it was reported that the driver had been cut in half by the steering wheel. Fifteen-year-olds don't forget details like that. My memory of the sound was haunting, even sickening. And yet—just a year or two later there I was blasting down the same hill, learning that even a '73 VW Fastback can do 120 with the aid of gravity. Kids, eh? Looking back, it's the wrecks I should have had, but somehow didn't, that scare me the most. It should have been me, sliced and diced by my own steering wheel.

I emerged from these years with the humble knowledge that I had cheated disaster on a number of occasions. What if I had killed a bystander or one of my friends? It was simple luck to escape alive and unmaimed, unjailed. These days I drive like Uncle Jessie, partially out of respect for my phenomenal luck as an idiot teen driver, partially because I know there is a whole new crop of them out there, ready to strike.

Sure, I was a particularly bad teen driver. Most aren't nearly so reckless. But let's just admit that child drivers smashing into and through things, killing themselves and their friends, is a freaky American tradition. We've set it up so the bloody automobile wreck is a rite of passage for American kids. How great is that? Exciting stuff for the kiddos. Unfortunately, these teenagers have no idea how vulnerable they are, how likely their predictably kid-like driving is to lead to a collision, or any concept of their own mortality. That's why they call 'em kids.

Generally speaking, high schoolers are horrible drivers. Study after study confirms what you always suspected: that the youngest drivers are by far the worst and most dangerous, the most likely to cause your untimely death. Of course, being teenagers, they think they've got it all figured out. The reality is they are far more likely to speed, tailgate, drive aggressively, and, ultimately, collide with foreign objects—four times more likely to crash than older drivers, according to the Insurance Institute for Highway Safety. When a group of rug rats occupies the same car, the likelihood of a wreck skyrockets even higher.

About a dozen sixteen-to-nineteen-year-olds are killed in wrecks every day, about four thousand to five thousand per year. Close to half a million go to emergency rooms each year after hitting something in their cars. (It happens that close to the same amount of bicyclists, of all ages, visit ERs each year in the United States.) And they take a lot of adults and fences and things with them, too. Today I noticed the cover of the latest *People* magazine, which stated, quite cryptically to someone who hasn't been following the latest missing-child news, "Where Is Carrie?" In a nation with magazine covers like that, the willingness to ignore a steady toll of thousands of violent kid deaths is curious.

A sizable portion of the problem of road safety comes down to kid drivers. What if we got rid of 'em all? Put them all in some kind of camp up in North Dakota? Ah, just kidding. What I mean, of course, is what if we kept them from driving for a few years? Take away their driver's licenses until they turn eighteen. Instead, they could ride bikes, walk, use transit, or sit in the passenger seat while someone with a more fully developed brain does the driving. Put 'em on bikes and thus take away their power to kill their friends and other road users. It sure would make us all safer, and it would make the kids healthier. Give 'em bike legs and eliminate the number one cause of death for young people in the United States.

It would save a lot of gas, too. That part gets people's attention. It's impossible to say how much gas kids use with their frivolous driving but it would seem to be as much as 10 percent of the country's daily fix, maybe around forty million gallons a day. In stark contrast to the strategy expressed in the mantra "drill, baby, drill," raising the legal driving age would actually have an immediate and powerful effect on the oil market. Maybe letting kids drive aimlessly around looking at other kids driving aimlessly around has something to do with why we feel the need to send other kids to fight wars in the desert.

Don't worry, kids. My associates inform me that this is a completely unrealistic proposal. You are way too in love with driving, your parents are way too busy to drive you to your job at TCBY, and the folks at the mall way too desperate for your idle dollars.

What's Good

I regard Henry Ford as my inspiration.

Adolph Hitler, 1931[31]

The American SUV boom came to an abrupt end in 2007. For a while there things were cooking right along. The accountants at Ford and GM had been gleaming over their companies' books for years, in between bouts of joyous *Riverdance* heel clicks. The 1990s were kind to them. Americans were in a veritable frenzy of buying pickup trucks and SUVs when gas was cheap. The most immediate problem facing the SUV business in the 1990s was the questionable roadworthiness of the vehicles after a spate of rollovers.

Then the oil market went rogue and the economy turned. By July 2008 prices for new light trucks and SUVs were down 20 percent on average as dealers tried to unload their overstock.[32] GM lost a shocking $38 billion in 2007. Ford reported a loss of $8.7 billion in the second quarter of '08; that stood as a record quarterly loss until General Motors reported theirs—$15.5 billion. Unbelievably, the car companies were losing more than the oil companies were making. Fire sale on

SUVs and pickups across the land. Then the financial crash of '08 arrived with nails for Detroit's coffin.

When the CEOs, former professed capitalists all, came to Washington with hats in hand in November 2008, the government bailout genie was already way out of the bottle. Why hold Detroit's feet over the fire for relative crumbs after absorbing over $300 billion of Citigroup's debt with no questions asked or strings attached? Earlier in the year Congress had already, somewhat quietly, floated a $25 billion loan to the automakers. Ostensibly, the companies were to use the money to meet short-term obligations and facilitate a wholesale transition to production of more sensible vehicles. As the volume of the begging grew to triple-digit decibel levels, Congress seemed intent on giving Detroit even more room at the trough.

There are all kinds of things that you have to more or less ignore to make a bailout of the auto industry seem remotely acceptable. For decades the automakers lobbied, quite successfully, against tougher mileage standards. *Keep the government out of Detroit's business!* they cried. *Let the market decide! The American people demand our huge gas guzzlers!* The auto companies fought like wolverines against tougher emissions and fuel efficiency standards, and failed to prepare for future challenges that were clearly apparent to the average college freshman, then begged for a lifeline when they finally, for complete lack of a better term, pulled their heads out. As soon as the market judges their enterprise negatively, the hypocrites spend millions trying to sell the notion that the market is broken. When the government is the only thing standing between them and the big sleep, suddenly the government isn't so evil after all.

Certainly Detroit has been at a disadvantage to foreign companies that have been making cars in the southern states with workers who are paid about half as much as those up north. The UAW is not blameless, but labor issues are not the fatal flaw. The fatal flaw has been Detroit's shortsighted focus on near-term profits at the expense of long-term viability. The American carmakers happily steered their businesses into positions of dependence on continued flow of cheap imported oil even as the warnings mounted that the cheap oil order could not last forever, and were completely caught out when consumers became more attracted (again) to smaller vehicles. They struggled, or perhaps declined, to match the quality of imports, and even jumped into the game of financing loans that could not be repaid, for the sake of short-term profits. For the sake of short-term profits, the American automakers were digging their own big grave out in the desert. The lack of vision they displayed in product development was nothing short of epic. Perhaps they acted this way because they knew that if and when sales cratered they would get bailed out.

It's not a surprise that Congress was able to slip $25 billion to Detroit and then slip them tens of billions more without raising many eyebrows around the country. The latest bailout of Detroit was really the continuation of a long-standing tradition, in which the U.S. government subsidizes the domestic auto industry to the detriment of the national interest.

Prior to World War II, the government stood lookout as a consortium of motorized interests, led by General

Motors, dismantled just about every one of the intra-urban rail systems in America, one by one. Many people today don't realize that extensive trolley and streetcar systems were running in cities across the nation in the early decades of the twentieth century. The transit companies struggled for many reasons, but their mass extinction wasn't entirely due to natural causes. They were disappeared. They were given the ol' concrete galoshes treatment, tracks torn up to make way for private autos and General Motors buses. The rails were expunged. The long-running scheme to kill rail transit was an egregious violation of the Sherman Antitrust Law, and GM was found guilty of criminal conspiracy by a federal grand jury. The punishment meted out by the government for this offense, however, did not begin to approach the level of a slap on the wrist.[33]

The free pass for GM was a reflection of the prevailing sentiment that "what's good for the country is good for General Motors, and vice versa." The quote comes from Charles Wilson, who served as GM's president from 1941 until 1953, when he was installed by Ike to head the Department of Defense.* Even today the president of GM could probably get away with making such a statement, unless he happened to say it in a roomful of folks who possess some knowledge of history, in which case he shouldn't be surprised to detect

---

*The oft-twisted quote is from Wilson's confirmation hearing before Congress. He was asked if he could, as secretary of defense, make a decision in the country's interest if he knew it would adversely affect his former company. The politically astute Wilson said that he could, but couldn't imagine such a situation arising.

some hearty chuckles if not outright guffaws. A look at the pre–World War II history of Ford and General Motors calls Wilson's whole happy premise into question. Not only did GM illegally bury the country's urban rail industry, both GM and Ford were heavily invested in Nazi Germany. Much of the equipment of the Nazi blitzkrieg was created in factories either partially or completely owned by Ford or GM. Battling the Germans, American soldiers were attacked by General Motors–built Opel bombers. Although the companies later insisted that they had severed their ties to the Nazis when the war started, documents have since been located which indicate that they controlled and continued their operations on behalf of the Nazis even after Hitler started rampaging around Europe, and perhaps even after he declared war on the United States. In the meantime the Detroit companies embarked on their role as Arsenal of Democracy with less than complete enthusiasm.[34] Was all this good for America? I think not. But how can you stay mad at a company that brings you the Pontiac Grand Am?

After the war the U.S. government embarked on a massive public works program to build superhighways. This idea seemed quite fine to Ike, who had been impressed by German autobahns while retaking Europe. Appropriations for the construction and maintenance of federal highways have been ongoing and increasing since then, and inspiring very little controversy the whole way. Federal highway expenditures climbed well into the hundreds of billions, which, until recently, seemed like a lot. Summer 2008 finally revealed the Achilles' heel of the Highway Trust Fund. Dependent on the federal gas tax, the fund shrank all of a sudden along with Americans' gasoline consumption after the oil spike. Few were offended—few noticed—when Congress transferred $8 billion from the general fund to make up for the shortfall.[35] It was, no doubt, only the first of many transfers to come. In addition to creating and maintaining much of the new infrastructure upon which cars and trucks would operate, the post–World War II government endeavored to pump up the suburban housing market by guaranteeing loans. These may not have been direct subsidies to the automakers, but they were indirect subsidies of unimaginable proportions, transforming the culture as well as the transportation system. As decisively as the Chinese communists chose bicycles, the American, uh, communists, fascists, corporatists, whatever you want to call them, chose cars.

Bailout Nation

By the summer of '79, Chrysler was about to kick off for good. In a country that chose cars, Chrysler was a failed car company facing bankruptcy. A helicopter drop from Uncle Sam was its only hope. After Congress and President Carter weighed the choices—dishing a few billion to the company (an unfathomable amount at the time) or letting it go belly-up to discharge its workforce onto the streets, where TV crews were waiting to record their folksy anti-Washington diatribes—the money got dished and the company lived on.

Chrysler recovered and eventually paid back its loan with interest, so the bailout has often been called a success. You won't be terribly surprised if I question that view. What, ultimately, was gained by saving Chrysler? The minivan? The K-car? No—obviously the most positive aspect of saving Chrysler was keeping actual Americans employed at nice-paying jobs, which is exactly what we needed then and still need now. But let's look at the big picture. Look what happened to Chrysler in the long run: It struggled, and it failed. It was consumed by Daimler, then the German company discreetly spit the half-chewed gristle back into its napkin, then it failed. Again. And then it was back begging for more money from the lender of last resort: your kids. This time the entire domestic auto industry was on life support—insolvent—and holding out its giant hand to the taxpayers, while discharging its workers onto the streets left and right. So much for paying back that $1.5 billion, eh? With interest, my ass.

Would it have been a better choice to let Chrysler go down in '79? It was hard to imagine all those folks losing their jobs, but look what's happening now. If we had let the failed business fail in '79, would this have helped the remaining domestic auto industry to grow richer, stronger, less clueless? We'll never know.

The big picture strongly suggests that the Chrysler bailout was a failure. If a few-billion-dollar bailout led to a $25 billion bailout one generation later, where will the $25 billion bailout lead? What kind of time bomb are we building for our kids? At what point are we better off pulling a Kevorkian on these hemorrhaging enterprises? Ack. The potential demise of industrial giants like Chrysler or even General Motors puts the American taxpayers in a tough spot. In addition to massive job losses (some estimate that one in every ten American jobs is "connected" to the auto industry), the loss of these companies could make the nation even more dependent on foreign patrons. At some point we might have to rely on foreign companies to supply our military vehicles, just like Hitler did. On the other hand, the *existence* of these companies has led to increased reliance on foreign patrons. The country's annual wealth transfer to petro-states swelled into the hundreds of billions as part-and-parcel of GM's and Ford's selling their SUVs like hotcakes, and now there is a waiting list for foreign-made hybrids while Detroit has nothing comparable to offer.

Anyway, disastrously poor business practices are now being rewarded with all you can eat at the public buffet. When you've got that kind of arrangement, who needs to set fires? Just pass the bacon.

Seriously, James Woolsey?

I have a bumper sticker on the back of my Prius that reads, BIN LADEN HATES THIS CAR.

James Woolsey, former CIA director[36]

Mr. Woolsey, sir, former CIA director, I hate to break it to you. It turns out that your Prius is not fighting the War on

Terror after all. Here's what your Prius is doing: slurping the Middle Eastern oil. That's right. It's not slurping as much as it could, sure, but slurp it does.

Sir, the fuel economy of your hybrid puts the Hummer and Ford Expulsion to shame; that's not exactly a news flash. It's still the most fuel-efficient car available in America as 2008 comes to its tumultuous end, according to the Environmental Protection Agency. Burning gasoline at the rate of about forty-five miles per gallon, however, a Prius is not achieving anything that hadn't been achieved by the garden-variety compacts of decades past. Remember the Geo Metro? European consumers can go out right now and purchase any one of a sizable assortment of cheap conventional diesel vehicles that would squash the Prius's mileage numbers, no battery pack required. The hybrid-electric's fuel economy is decidedly unspectacular. Slurp.

If every driver of a gas-powered car in America were suddenly forced to switch to a hybrid-electric vehicle (HEV)—say, if Ed Begley Jr. seized the reins of power in a bloody coup d'etat—we would still be dependent on imported oil and subject to the violent whims of the oil markets. There are degrees of dependence like there are degrees of death. Doubling the efficiency of the auto fleet could not break this dependence, as upwards of 70 percent of our daily fix arrives from some other country.[37]

Many nonetheless see the hybrid as a waypoint, a beacon of hope along the road to a sustainable future. The danger with this half-measure is that, instead of showing us the way to a brighter world, it might guide us into a dead-end alley and seal our fate. It's certainly conceivable that this country, a decade or two down the line and using only high-mileage cars like the Prius, could find itself even more oil-dependent and in a much bigger predicament than it is today. There is no telling what might happen with supply issues or many other factors affecting markets in the future, while the maximum potential benefits of high-mileage cars are known and limited. If the nation is unable or unwilling to imagine fundamental changes in its driving habits, the only sure way to get out from under this dilemma is to switch fuels.

Mister Woolsey, you've been double-crossed. Your Prius is not part of the solution; it's still part of the problem. Bin Laden thinks it quite fine.

Sir, you're probably feeling a lot of confusion and anger right now. That's perfectly normal. Know that you are not alone. That same overwhelming sense of betrayal that you feel is familiar to tens of dozens of distraught hybrid owners who, like you, dared to peel back the veil and look at the big picture. There is even a name for your emptiness: post-Prius depression syndrome. They're working on a pill.

Half Measures

James Woolsey didn't express any interest in helping the environment with his Toyota, only a belief that he was antagonizing terrorist kingpins with it. Others are under the impression that driving a hybrid vehicle is a real positive for Mother Earth.

There are prime parking spaces right next to the front door of the local grocery store, right next to the handicap spots; signs indicate these spaces are reserved for "environmentally friendly" vehicles. It's a well-intentioned gesture, maybe, but it is also ridiculous. In fact, I'd say it's a glaring symptom of our national disease. The stupid parking spaces may be harmless, but the willful ignorance they betray is certainly not.

Okay, people, let's get this straight. Your Prius is not environmentally friendly. It may be relatively environmentally friendly compared to other vehicles sold in the United States, but that really isn't much to boast about. The purchaser and user of a new HEV, the person who chooses to travel around town accompanied by three thousand pounds of metal and plastic and a huge battery pack filled with metallic mash, is not doing the environment any favors. Every day your Prius will consume something like fifty times its own weight in organic material that has been condensed over hundreds of millions of years into crude oil, then turned into gasoline. It's a wildly extravagant use of energy. Every Toyota Prius that pops out of a factory, complete with its two engines, is an incredibly elaborate conglomeration of parts manufactured and gathered from around the world at great environmental cost. The plant in Canada that processes all the nickel for Prius batteries is one of the worst producers of acid rain on the planet. After its estimated ten-year lifespan, the battery becomes toxic waste. Over the life of the vehicle, from development through disposal, the relatively complex hybrid will carry a total environmental cost that will approach and could actually exceed that of a much larger, conventional gas-hogging vehicle.[38] What about emissions, you ask? Sure, the hybrid puts out a smaller portion of the same nasty stuff that regular cars produce. But half of a poison cloud is still too much. There's no cause for rejoicing there, nothing to be very proud about.

The Prius people who are excited about their car's green credentials remind me of the time I bought a rotten bratwurst for half price. I was quite hungry, delivering packages around the city on my bike, and the guy at the hot dog stand was all out of bratwurst. Except this one over here, he said, which is quite old. "I give you half price!" he barked. That's how I learned that half price for rotten bratwurst is still a bad deal.

People are to be commended for making positive changes, trying to do the right thing. The Prius drivers may be rolling in the right direction, but they're still squarely in negative territory. They're not to the point where they can pull over and give each other pats on the back. Somewhere along the line they lost track of a basic truth: Their HEVs still consume plenty of fuel and spew plenty of fumes, and this is not good, but bad for the environment. In fact, driving one is closer to a whirlwind orgy of consumption than an ecological coup. It's rotten bratwurst all the way. No green buttons, and no national security merit badges, given out for that. We will reserve our badges and buttons for those who actually stop transporting themselves in ways that harm the environment and national security: Those who move under their own power. These are the only true transportation patriots.

In reality, only those of us who consume zero petroleum can preach to everybody else about the evils of oil. Is there any such individual? Perhaps in the African bush or beneath the canopy of the Amazon rainforest there are still some people living virtually petroleum-free existences. Here in the U.S. we are all junkies, even the patriotic folks who move about under their own power.

In the United States, less than half the oil consumed is burned by passenger vehicles. The rest goes into moving freight, heating homes, and creating an impossibly wide array of commercial items from which we all tend to benefit. Even though she travels under her own power and thus consumes almost no liquid fuel for transportation purposes, the bicyclist is not somehow living off the grid, exempt from oil. Taking part in the spectacle of America, the bicyclist is intertwined in this historic liquid petroleum–driven lifestyle, even if she never drives. The computers and keyboards, the heat in her home, the fabric of her backpack, the lube on her chain, the mail, the magic pills, the cops and ambulances at the ready, the contact lenses, the *food and water*—it all depends to some degree on liquid petroleum. Often it depends entirely on liquid petroleum. Often it *is* liquid petroleum, molded into chairs and computer parts and trash bags and undershirts. Carbon forks. The aluminum or steel bicycle frame could not exist without the explosive petroleum that powers the big engines at the mines. It wouldn't get to the local shop from China (the vast majority are created in China) without the smoke-belching cargo ships. So let's not get too smug, wheelmen. And if we ever do create this renewable energy economy, even that will depend on petroleum for its very existence. Bow down to your master, America. There is no escape from oil, not even on the silent, elusive bicycle.

Plug In, Tune Out

In fairness to Mr. Woolsey, he's put a great deal of work into making his Prius habit more truly green in recent years. He turned the car into a plug-in hybrid; that is, he modified it so he can charge the car's battery from a regular electrical outlet, and thus can drive for much longer distances without burning any liquid fuel. Even better, he put solar panels on his house, so the electricity he uses to charge the car is from a clean source. Bin Laden might not be so giddy at the thought of this improved Prius.

Toyota and GM (if it survives long enough) are on track to bring plug-ins to mass market before 2012. Unfortunately, unlike James Woolsey's, these plug-in hybrids will most likely still be running substantially on fossil fuels. They will still burn some gasoline, and the power they suck from the outlet will most likely originate from a coal- or natural gas–fired plant.[39]

Ideally we'd transition far, far away from coal and develop a solar- and wind-power infrastructure with enough girth to handle the tremendous load from a fleet of fully electric plug-in vehicles recharging every night—that's a lot of joules, Verne—in addition to the normal ridiculously heavy load that already exists. Realistically we'll need to ramp up the nuclear, too, many will say. This is the new American Dream—to create a renewable energy infrastructure to power the American fleet in all its glory, such that the American Way of Life won't miss a beat. The building of this new infrastructure is the new "Manhattan Project" that is often mentioned these days, implying a determined and coordinated push by government and private enterprise to fundamentally transform electric power production into something less deadly in the long term, and use it to power a business-as-usual brand of guilt-free driving. So far the project, though almost universally endorsed, has remained primarily in the realm of imaginary things. Real renewable energy needs more than nudges here and there and happy talk from the public sector. It will require unfaltering commitment from a government that, so far, has shown no signs of fighting its way out of this paper bag. Look at the directions government has been pushing in the past several years: Ethanol mandates and subsidies, hydrogen fuel cells,* huge tax credits for purchasing hybrid half-measure vehicles, huger credits for purchasing Hummers, proposals to sue OPEC and temporarily suspend gas taxes,

---

*Some folks will remain attached to the seductive notion of a hydrogen economy for some time but, as Ulf Bossel explains, it's a non-starter. "Because of the high energy losses within a hydrogen economy the synthetic energy carrier cannot compete with electricity. As the fundamental laws of physics cannot be changed by research, politics or investments, a hydrogen economy will never make sense." In other words, it makes no sense to waste energy liberating hydrogen from water to create a fuel cell to power a vehicle when the vehicle can be powered directly with the same electricity, ultimately using about one quarter the amount of energy.[40]

"drill, baby, drill," making the Detroit CEOs give up their corporate jets—the folks in Washington have been offering one embarrassment of a proposal after another. Can we really imagine them pulling it together and winning the game with a three-pointer at the buzzer? It's going to be a challenge.

At some point we will actually have to slough off our half-measures and blubbering dead-end runs into back alleys and start this new Manhattan Project that everybody's been talking about. If we don't start, I'm pretty sure it won't get done. And once we start, we'll have to be headed in the right direction, or we could very easily end up farther away from our goal than before we started. But our motivation to begin the mission slip-slides away with the price of oil.

The more we understand about this colossal project, the further it recedes into the future. Reality keeps stomping on the dream. When it comes time to replace it, the people suddenly begin to understand and appreciate the energy density of gasoline. The slowly dawning realization that there is no real substitute for the magic juice spawns anger, denial, desperation, all that good stuff.

VIII

REASONS TO RIDE

The Flying Machine*

ORVILLE WAS MORE EXCITED THAN WILBUR ABOUT BICYCLING. As the safety-bike craze swept the country in 1892, Orville plunked down $160 for a new Columbia. Wilbur bought a used Eagle at an auction. Orv raced his Columbia on the track, whereas Will was known as a "wonderful fancy skater and the best performer in Dayton on a horizontal bar."[1] Both thought they could make a living off bicycles, and the boys immediately opened a shop together. They became bicycle dealers, mechanics, and manufacturers.

Inside every one of the primal motorcars was the beating heart of a bicycle, and bicycles strongly influenced the development of flying machines as well. The Wrights' various developmental aircraft at Kitty Hawk used several different

---

*The elder Maxim, Hiram Stevens Maxim, inventor of the fully automatic machine gun, also tried his hand at creating flying machines. In 1894 he tested a crazy-looking 3.5-ton contraption powered by steam engines. The beast actually lifted off, but like many other early versions of the airplane, there was no hope of controlling it in the air until the Wrights figured it out.

types of bicycle parts in their construction—hubs as a sort of landing gear, spokes in the wings, chains and gears driving the propellers. More important to the Wrights' success than any bicycle part, however, was their understanding of the unique physics involved in riding one.

Engrossed in solving the mystery of flight, the Wrights naturally became obsessed with the observation and study of birds. Wilbur chased birds along the coast, taking highly detailed notes—the slight twisting of the wings, the oscillation of the birds' bodies when gliding in for landings, details most people would never notice. In the same way the Wrights worked to understand the subtler aspects of the physics of bicycle riding, which were also mysterious and obscure. Their experience with and observation of bicycle balance and steering, and the ever curious phenomenon of counter-steering, helped them become the first to grasp the need for multidimensional controls in a flying machine. They understood that controlled flight would depend on the same sort of continuous readjustment that the bicyclist—or the gymnast or skater for that matter—uses to maintain balance.[2] Figuring out why and how to control the craft as it hurtled through the air was arguably the most important of the Wrights' many contributions to the development of the airplane, and this came substantially from their familiarity with bicycles.

At the risk of sounding absurd, riding a bike is a bit like flying. Diving into a turn on a bicycle provides a delightful floating sensation. The body is hurtling through the air, suspended above the ground on a minimal framework of steel and wheels. Floating on air, or at least, air-filled tires. The machine itself, if it is a lightweight bicycle, accounts for a small portion of the total weight of the bicycle-rider system. The vehicle is made up mostly of rider, who leans into a turn as would a bird.

This sensation is unique to bicycling. It's not available to drivers of four-wheeled vehicles; they enjoy a different set of thrills, to be sure, but not that one. It's not even available to motorcyclists. Due to the comparably immense mass of the machine and the low center of gravity, a motorcycle in a turn has a much less dynamic, lively feel than a bicycle. Avid motorcyclists who also ride bicycles report that the sensation of riding a motorcycle at 145 miles per hour is similar to the sensation of riding a bicycle at 45 miles per hour. The motorcycle provides a much more solid ride, not necessarily an advantage to the low-budget thrill-seeker.

Adventure

The average citizen of New York, unless he is a long-distance cyclist or the owner of one or more excellent horses, is likely to have a very limited knowledge of the remarkable extent and variety of scenery which may be found within a few miles of this city.

New York Times, 1902[3]

When he became obsessed with the horseless carriage, Hiram Maxim was an enthusiastic member of Pope's League of

American Wheelmen who had "studied every route in the entire road book in detail." He was not unlike many folks whom we might pass out on the road today, exploring their world via bicycle. Later Maxim used this same LAW guidebook to find his way back from his motoring adventures in unfamiliar territory.

Maxim loved an adventure. That much is clear. He relished the earliest days of auto development, the "horseless carriage days," when he and his wisecracking assistant would set out into the hinterlands to shock-test their primal car and bedazzle the populace. Bogging down in the sand, gearbox dropping into the road, cylinders glowing red in the dark, waking up the local blacksmith to fashion strange bits, having to stash the broken machine and take the train home—not getting there was half the fun. Some of these early road tests were more reminiscent of mountain bike epics through a third world country than car trips through the American countryside.

Maxim loved working out the kinks of the motor-carriage better than he loved the end product. They were shooting for a machine that could take the most ham-handed operator anywhere over rough roads, one that would keep running as long as there was fuel dripping into the engine. Realization of the goal left him curiously unsatisfied. The journey was worth much more than the pot of gold at the end.

In the 1930s an aged Maxim wrote dreamily of air travel and wondered where it might lead. "History has a strange way of repeating itself," he reminds his twentieth- and twenty-first-century readers, meaning that another wholesale revolution in transportation could be right around the corner, and we might not see it coming. But looking forward to the next revolution or remembering the last one is not nearly as thrilling as being in it, man.

And here's Maxim's B. B. King speech—The thrill is gone, the thrill is gone away:

> There is one thing which I regret. It is that the thrill I experienced when I rode my bicycle from Salem to Lynn that summer night in the long ago has gone. I used to dream of skimming over the country highways, up hill and down dale, with no effort except that of steering. Today the ability to do this is taken for granted; a motor trip has become as prosaic as a ride in a railroad train. All the hopes and ambitions of 1893 have been realized; but with their realization the sparkle and the thrill have departed.[4]

No word on whether Maxim took the next logical step and rediscovered his love for bicycle riding.

Tyranny of the Bus

Let's just admit it. If you have to be in it, doing it, if you are beholden to it, mass transit sucks. It's another thing to be planning for it, idealizing it, dreaming about it, even paying for it. But if you rely on mass transit to get places, that is not freedom.

Light-rail systems, once disappeared by the GM consortium, are back in vogue around the nation, reanimated, and on balance this is a good thing. Urban commuters are enjoying the nineteenth-century light-rail experience and putting it to good use—often driving to the rail station in a private car. I am a believer that these intra-city systems need to be rebuilt and intercity passenger rail needs to be expanded. There is an insidious trade-off at work with any rail system, however. As it works for you, you end up working for it, hustling off to meet departure times, watching the minutes and seconds. That's a clock-watching style of mobility that was dust-binned by the invention of the bicycle, which freed mankind from the rails. Stepping onto a train is like stepping into the time before the bicycle was invented.

The urban bus system, brought to you in a sense by General Motors, is still worse. The city bus is a mess. In Denver there is the Number 15 bus, which runs up and down Colfax Avenue, the longest continuous commercial strip in the world. Riding the 15 will be uneventful, most likely. Most likely. Don't be too surprised if you get infected with smallpox, though. The odds of being urinated upon are also fairly strong.

Those who are beholden to the 15 are likely to notice ongoing deterioration in the quality of their bus-riding experience. Officials at RTD, Denver's mass transit authority, noted during the energy spike of 2007-08 that their operation was losing $100,000 for every penny rise in the price of diesel. At the same time the sales tax revenue that supported the transit system was falling. While RTD's bottom line was being ravaged in this way, the citizenry was growing more dependent on the buses and trains.[5] The same pattern was evident in cities across the country. Some have called it a death spiral. The buses get increasingly sucky, more crowded and more expensive to ride—while the service slows and deteriorates due to lack of funding.

Disgruntled and occasionally urinated upon, bus riders are as primed as anyone could possibly be to make the switch to bicycling. The 15 is like a little rolling factory, churning out new cycle commuters. Kind of like those mobile weapons factories that were alleged to exist in Saddam's Iraq.

The liberal city-dwellers who have loved mass transit for decades, with votes and words, have not been at its mercy. Those who are tend to arrive at different conclusions, but then again, those who are at the mercy of transit are generally not to be found in the upper reaches of government or otherwise gripping the levers of power. They need the bus but they start to resent it. My own anti-bus tendencies are a product of my having had to use it—or so I felt at the time—for quite a while. At some point I reached for the freedom of the bicycle, so obvious in retrospect.

When bus patrons switch to human power, it doesn't do a great deal of good for society at large. It will bring down health care costs but won't save any gas or prevent any toxic spewings. However, it does a world of good for the individuals making the switch. When I switched from the bus to the bike for my trip to work, I felt like Spartacus breaking off the iron shackles. It was one of the best changes I have ever made. And unlike Spartacus, who walked his army of escaped slaves all up and down the Italian peninsula, hemmed in by the Alps on one side and the ocean on the other, I experienced no critical deficiency of available transportation after breaking the chains.

Two Birds

It doesn't much matter what exercise you take, provided it involves the leg muscles in particular and suits you in age, strength, aptitude, and experience.

Dr. Paul Dudley White[6]

I don't like killing birds. I don't even like to think about other people killing birds. So naturally I regard the phrase "kill two birds with one stone" somewhat negatively. People say it as if it's a good thing. Hey, I eliminated two birds there, and used but one stone. What's with this bizarre hatred of birds? And are stones really that valuable?

Anyway, it turns out that this unfortunate phrase is useful to describe the utility of the bicycle. Riding a bike kills two birds. It may be helpful to think of these birds as horrid evil buzzards that deserve to die.

(Actually, bicycling simultaneously kills many more birds than two. It's like a bird massacre out there. But we'll just concentrate on the two biggest birds for now.)

The first bird is simple and boring: It gets you from here to there. The miracle of mechanized transport. The second bird is the nifty one: It provides exercise that is critical to human health. Efficient transportation and exercise. At the same time. We would take either one of these on its own and be grateful, but both together? It's completely brilliant.

As we've seen, there is some extra danger involved in bicycling, a pattern of minor injury caused by the unique properties and challenges of the machine. And yes, some extra danger on the upper end of the injury scale, too; probably even a slightly elevated risk of death by collision relative to driving. Even when accounting for this extra danger, however, the act of bicycling has proved itself to be incredibly healthy. A British researcher, Mayer Hillman, found the health benefits of bicycling to outweigh the much celebrated risks by twenty to one.[7] Researchers studying a group of factory workers found that the regular bicyclists among them were as fit, on average, as non-bicycling factory workers who were ten years younger.[8] What it comes down to is this: If you exercise, you're much less likely to get some horrible disease or have a heart attack and die.[9] And bicycling is good exercise.

Physical activity has also been shown to be important to mental health. Strenuous exercise gives less-than-stable individuals like myself a means to dispose of excess stress, to burn it up in the body's engine. This, in turn, keeps me sane, or at least in sane's ballpark. Dr. Paul Dudley White, who cared for President Ike after his heart attack, was another who believed in this power of exercise to affect mental faculties. Forty years ago he wrote, "Physical fitness includes the health of the brain … physical labor is one of the best antidotes, perhaps the best, for emotional stress or mental fatigue."[10] People thought

Dr. White was a bit off the deep end, but the regular bicyclist understands exactly what he was getting at.

Humans need exercise just as they need sleep, food, and adventure. It doesn't have to be bicycling, but it has to be something. The consequences of not exercising are far more dire than the consequences of bicycling in traffic.

America has been going downhill. The citizens are working harder and longer, and off hours are more likely to be spent in front of a television or computer screen, scarfing Cheetos. Obesity is epidemic. Spare tires have grown in an inverse relationship to spare time. This presents a dilemma, but thankfully one with an easy solution. If you need to exercise, and you need to get around, why not do both at the same time? Kill two birds. With apologies to my bird friends.

One Thousand Miles per Gallon

Using a scientist's definition of efficiency, the human machine is not much more efficient than the typical gasoline engine. Neither does very well in that each converts less than a quarter of its intake of fuel energy into work, wasting the rest. However, despite its notoriously unreliable and inefficient engine, the bicycle-and-rider is the unsurpassed efficiency star among transport modes. In terms of energy use per passenger mile, nothing can carry its jock.

The fuel used in bicycling is, of course, derived from various forms of animal and plant matter. A transportational bicyclist will require just slightly more of the same animal and plant matter that a sedentary person uses for everyday living. And the fuel used for driving comes from various forms of animal and plant matter as well, although in a very different form. Petroleum energy is highly concentrated compared to food energy, but they are both, for transportation's sake, energy. To compare the two, measurements of the energy in food and in liquid petroleum can both be reduced to the same units. There are quite a few kilocalories' worth of energy packed into a gallon of gasoline. About thirty-one thousand kilocalories per gallon, actually. (A kilocalorie is the equivalent of what is commonly and mistakenly referred to as a calorie.) Comparing gasoline's kilocalories to the range consumed in exercise, we find that a bicyclist could easily achieve the equivalent of one thousand miles per gallon, even at a relatively brisk pace.[11] The most fuel-efficient car available for widespread consumption in America—our old friend Mr. Prius—would have to consume more than twenty times as much energy as the bicyclist to move its driver the same distance, even at bicycling speeds. Slurp.

The fatal energy flaw of the Prius, as with any car, is its weight. Every time James Woolsey drives himself to the golf course, his Prius has to haul not only James Woolsey but itself. While it requires very little energy for a motor to move a human, moving the three-thousand-pound contraption surrounding the human is a major production. A tiny percentage of the energy in gasoline is used to move the driver. The vast majority is wasted, and almost all of the rest is used to move the weight of the machine.

Even when the Prius evolves into a fully electric plug-in green machine, weaned from the petroleum teat, driving it will still be inordinately consumptive of energy and tremendously inefficient compared to riding a bicycle. Conversely, the bicycle-and-rider amplifies the human engine's power with levers and gears and wheels, while adding very little extra weight. Human legs that pack only a tiny fraction of the Prius's punch still have more than enough to move the bicycle-and-rider at speed.

The traveler on foot doesn't require or consume much energy either, but the pedestrian is hampered by his lack of wheels. Without the benefit of the bicycle's mechanical advantage, the poor sod on foot will consume the same amount of energy as a bicyclist traveling four times as fast.[12] As a long-time bicyclist and pedestrian, I am keenly aware of the relative inefficiency of the walking motion, putting one foot in front of the other. Halting, unsmooth, slow. Rolling is a massive improvement.

Nothing—not commuter rail, biofuel buses, Prii, or pedestrians—can approach the efficiency of the bicycle. Bicycling stands completely above other transportation modes in that regard. We can see that we promote these modes of transportation, while trumpeting the critical importance of increasing efficiency, in inverse proportion to their efficiency. That would seem to be, a bit, inefficient.

Drive Less, Live More

It's become fairly apparent that the dependence we face in America is not so much a dependence on oil, but a dependence on driving itself. Now, I'm going to suggest something crazy here. Drive less. Whoa. Told you it was crazy.

Notice I didn't say travel less. Heck, travel more. Travel to your heart's content. What I'm saying is do more of your traveling in a mode that adds life rather than takes it away. Whatever mode you choose, make sure it gets you where you need to go in good time, but also choose a mode that makes you stronger and happier, that makes your soul smile and your spirit fly. If you can find a way to add some adventure to a mundane daily commute, I suggest you do that. Life is too short, my friends.

Sure enough, America seems to be figuring this out. If I'm here to tell people to start riding bikes, the uncertainty over future energy supplies, or the perfection of the machine, or *something*, is already doing that job, and doing it better than any one pedal-pushing, keyboard-tapping guy ever could. This positive trend won't kill the energy monster, but it will rock the personal world of anyone who takes up bicycling for transportation, as they drive less, and live more.

ACKNOWLEDGMENTS

Special thanks to Scott Adams at FalconGuides for helping to visualize and push another one of my books into existence. Scott has been my number one advocate in the publishing world.

The contract was signed in the summer of 2008 when the price of oil was near its dizzying heights for the year. As I wrote from August to November events were unfolding with breathtaking speed and world-changing magnitude. It proved difficult or impossible to keep up. Thanks to John Burbidge and any other editor whose life I made more difficult with last-second changes and other infuriating what-not.

Thanks very much to my wife Christie who was beyond patient with me for the past several months, and to my good friends at work who helped pick up my slack.

The history here is based primarily on the writings of some notable bicyclists of the past—Hiram Percy Maxim, Frances Willard, Major Taylor, and a few others—and newspaper articles from the period. Secondary sources were numerous, but particularly important were Andrew Ritchie's biography of Major Taylor and Jim Fitzpatrick's *The Bicycle in Wartime*. On the subject of energy, Matt Simmons's *Twilight in the Desert* proved to be the most useful source. Although Simmons has been busted for some hysterical-sounding predictions that he made at the height of the 2008 oil spike, his careful look at the knowns and unknowns of Saudi production capacity remains the most important work on oil available in the mass market. I have also been influenced by the writings of Ulf Bossel, Robert Rapier, Robert Hirsch, Dani Rodrick, and others in varying degrees.

Apologies to all who feel misrepresented or offended by the pronouncements herein. This is a book composed largely of the rantings of one dude who happens to have ridden a hell of a lot of miles on his bicycle. For better or worse he has arrived at some conclusions that differ from the conventional wisdom. As such, much of the book could be viewed as highly objectionable.

Thanks for reading, and I hope you enjoyed it.

NOTES

I: Interesting Times

1. David Brooks, "The Coming Age of Activism," *New York Times*, 18 July 2008.

II: Circle of Power

1. Hiram Maxim, *Horseless Carriage Days* (New York: Harper and Brothers, 1936), 3.
2. John Rae, *American Automobile Manufacturers* (Philadelphia: Chilton and Company, 1959), 7.
3. Allan Nevins, *Ford: The Times, the Man, the Company* (New York: Charles Scribner's Sons, 1954), 92-93.
4. Maxim, *Horseless Carriage Days*, 4.
5. John Ingham, *Biographical Dictionary of American Business Leaders* (Westport, Conn.: Greenwood Publishing Group, 1983), 1107-8.
6. "Gossip of the Cyclers," *New York Times*, 28 August 1898.
7. "Saved from Potter's Field," *New York Times*, 27 May 1893. "Bicycle Riders Locked Up," *New York Times*, 7

September 1893, in which the NYPD is seen jailing a woman for riding without a light. The *Times* editorial appeared on 31 May 1893.

8. Colonel Pope is given credit for passage of similar laws elsewhere: "He assumed the cost of test cases between cyclists and various city governments, with the result that bicycles were soon admitted to city parks and boulevards on the same basis as carriages and other vehicles." (Ingham, *Biographical Dictionary of American Business Leaders*, 1107-8.)

9. Maxim, *Horseless Carriage Days*, 49.

10. Ambrose Bierce, *The Devil's Dictionary* (New York: Neale Publishing Company, 1911; Mineola, N.Y.: Dover Publications, 1993), 64.

11. Nevins, *Ford*, 149.

12. Ibid., 156.

13. Ibid., 161. Nevins cites William Simonds, *Henry Ford* (Overland Park: F. Clymer, 1946). Simonds is not considered a rock-solid source, but Nevins is, generally.

14. "Eddie Has Flown," *Boulder Daily Camera*, 2 December 1895. Having lived in Boulder for many years (long ago), I have taken some creative license with the description of the countryside and Kiefer's route.

15. *Boulder Daily Camera*, 12 November 1895. No article title given.

16. "Accused of Arson," *New York Times*, 29 July 1897.

17. "Pope Bicycle Building Burned," *New York Times*, 13 March 1896.

18. Incidents found while browsing through the archives of the *New York Times*.

19. Pickering Walker, *The Wagonmasters* (Norman: University of Oklahoma Press, 1966), 236.

20. Maria Ward, *Bicycling for Ladies* (New York: Brentano's, 1896), 12.

21. "The Pleasures of Bicycling," *Outing*, April 1890, 78. "Colorado Briefs," *Colorado Transcript*, 13 January 1897, 2.

22. "The Color Line Declared," *New York Times*, 21 February 1894. It should be noted that many delegates dissented eloquently, but were outnumbered.

23. Lynn Tolman, "League Rights a Wrong, Lifting Forgotten Racial Ban," *Worcester Telegram and Gazette*, 30 May 1999.

III: The Next Big Thing

1. Andrew Ritchie, *Major Taylor: The Extraordinary Career of a Champion Bicycle Racer* (Baltimore: Johns Hopkins University Press, 1996), 90.

2. Marshall Taylor, *The Fastest Bicycle Rider in the World: The Story of a Colored Boy's Indomitable Courage and Success against Great Odds* (Worcester: Wormley Publishing, 1928), 1.

3. Cited in Ritchie, *Major Taylor*, 95.

4. Taylor, *The Fastest Bicycle Rider in the World*, 41.

5. "Trouble on Taunton's Track," *New York Times*, 24 September 1897.

6. "Gossip of the Cyclers," *New York Times*, 3 October 1897. Despite the *Times*' tone here, Taylor was generally happy with his treatment by the newspapers and regarded the press as an ally in his war against prejudice. Much of

his autobiography is composed of lengthy outtakes from newspaper articles.

7. Taylor, *The Fastest Bicycle Rider in the World,* 100-1.
8. Ibid., 126-32.
9. "Trouble at Cycle Race," *New York Times,* 30 July 1901, 5.
10. "Cycle Racer Attacked Rival," *New York Times,* 22 August 1901.
11. Peter Nye, *Hearts of Lions* (New York: W. W. Norton and Company, 1988), 82.
12. Ibid., 95-96.
13. "Cooper Won Ten-Mile Race," *New York Times,* 27 August 1901, 3.
14. Allan Nevins, *Ford: The Times, the Man, the Company* (New York: Charles Scribner's Sons, 1954), 205. Nevins cites the *Detroit Journal,* 11 October 1901, as reporting that Cooper and Oldfield got "scarcely a ripple of applause."
15. Ibid., 204. Nevins cites the *Detroit Tribune,* 11 October 1901.
16. *Detroit Free Press,* 16 March 1902.
17. Nevins, *Ford,* 204-14.
18. Bryan Ford, *Clara: Mrs. Henry Ford* (Detroit: Wayne State University Press, 2002), 76.
19. Ibid., 76.
20. William Sturm, "Wide Open All the Way, Part One," *Saturday Evening Post,* 19 September 1925, 56, 61.
21. John Ingham, *Biographical Dictionary of American Business Leaders* (Westport, Conn.: Greenwood Publishing Group, 1983), 1108.

22. "Auto Cooper Raced With Ran by the Victim," *New York Times*, 21 November 1906. "Third Man in Auto Wreck," *New York Times*, 22 November 1906, reports that there were not three but four others in the Matheson with Cooper, in which case there were two survivors.
23. Ritchie, *Major Taylor*, 205-57. Later Frank Schwinn paid to have Taylor's body exhumed and moved to a nicer part of the cemetery with a statue and plaque.

IV: Uses

1. *Boulder Daily Camera*, 13 November 1894, reprint from *Hardware* magazine.
2. "Bike to the Klondike," *Essex County (N.Y.) Republican*, 19 August 1897.
3. "Gossip of the Wheelmen," *New York Times*, 6 October 1895.
4. "The War Bicycle," *New York Times*, 30 September 1894.
5. The fully automatic machine gun, of course, was invented by Maxim's father. See a picture of the Pope death bike in Jim Fitzpatrick, *The Bicycle in Wartime: An Illustrated History* (Washington: Brassey's, 1998), 33.
6. Amir Moghaddaas Eesfehani, "The Bicycle's Long Way to China: The Appropriation of Cycling as a Foreign Cultural Technique, 1860-1940," in *Cycle History 13*, ed. Andrew Ritchie and Nicholas Clayton (San Francisco: Cycle Publishing, 2003).
7. Masanobu Tsuji, *Japan's Greatest Victory, Britain's Worst*

Defeat, trans. Margaret Lake (New York: Da Capo Press, 1997), 151.

8. The information for this section is taken primarily from the chapter "The Bicyclists" in ibid., 149-51.
9. Fitzpatrick, *The Bicycle in Wartime*, 136.
10. For example, see Major-General S. Woodburn Kirby, *Singapore: The Chain of Disaster* (New York: Macmillan Company, 1971), which doesn't mention bicycles or Colonel Tsuji.
11. Tsuji, *Japan's Greatest Victory, Britain's Worst Defeat*, 32.
12. Fitzpatrick, *The Bicycle in Wartime*, 75. The photograph of Paris after the war can be seen in this book as well, pages 150-51.
13. Jim Dwyer, "City is Rebuffed in Its Effort to Block Monthly Mass Bike Rides," *New York Times*, 16 February 2006. The article notes that the NYPD has a habit of infiltrating rides with officers in disguise, knowledge of which must have an interesting effect on the social dynamic within the group.
14. Colin Moynihan, "A Blue Ross 10-Speed Isn't Hard to Find; a Bomber Who Rode It Is," *New York Times*, 15 March 2008. Construction workers found an old Ross 10-speed in the trash the morning after an Army recruitment station was bombed and reported it to police. The police seem to have proceeded from that point onward under the dubious assumption that the poor trashed Ross was the same bike used in the crime.
15. Special Bulletin of the Denver Police Department. Revealed in a press conference by the local chapter of the

American Civil Liberties Union, 21 August 2008. During convention week bicyclists made the Terrorist Watch List.

16. Murray Weiss and Lukas Alpert, "Hunt for the Bicycle Bomber," *New York Post*, 7 March 2008. This article notes that the presumed bomber was seen "peddling" away from the scene. Ah, he should have been easy to catch then.

17. Al Baker, "In Times Square Blast, Echoes of Earlier Bombings," *New York Times*, 7 March 2008.

V: The Aliens

1. National Bicycle Dealers' Association statistics. Their numbers are dependent largely on estimates. http://nbda.com/page.cfm?pageID=34.

2. "Brief Bicycle Notes," *Essex County (N.Y.) Republican*, 18 August 1897.

3. "Among the Wheelmen," *New York Times*, 4 September 1893.

4. Peter Nye, *Hearts of Lions* (New York: W. W. Norton and Company, 1988), 99.

5. "Don'ts for the Wheelman," *Boulder Daily Camera*, 1895.

6. Willard's 1895 work *Wheel within a Wheel* is reprinted as *How I Learned to Ride the Bicycle: Reflections of an Influential 19th Century Woman* (Sunnyvale, Calif.: Fair Oaks Publishing, 1991), 75.

VI: Challenges of the Wheel

1. Frances Willard, *How I Learned to Ride the Bicycle: Reflections of an Influential 19th Century Woman* (Originally titled *Work within a Wheel*; Sunnyvale, Calif.: Fair Oaks Publishing, 1991), 31.
2. Ibid., 72.
3. From the inauguration speech of Franklin Delano Roosevelt, 4 March 1933.
4. Ken Kifer, September 2001 Bicycle Safety Survey. www.kenkifer.com/bikepages/survey/sept01.htm.
5. William Moritz, "Adult Bicyclists in the United States: Characteristics and Riding Experience in 1996." www.bicyclinglife.com/Library/Moritz2.htm.
6. For an international perspective see Eero Pasanen, "The Risks of Bicycling." Doctor Pasanen's analysis of data from Scandinavia is available on John Allen's Web site: www.bikexprt.com/research/pasanen/helsinki.htm#abstract.
7. Insurance Institute for Highway Safety.
8. Peter Jacobsen, "Safety in Numbers: More Walkers and Bicyclists, Safer Walking and Bicycling," *Injury Prevention* 9 (2003): 205-9.
9. Insurance Institute for Highway Safety, "Bicycle Fatality Facts 2006." www.iihs.org/research/fatality_facts_2006/bicycles.html.
10. Insurance Institute for Highway Safety.
11. The most enthusiastic promoters of Jacobsen's theory have been those concerned with the negative effects of helmet compulsion and advocates looking for support for

programs designed to increase cycling mode share. For a direct response to and extension of Jacobsen's article, see Dorothy Robinson, "Safety in Numbers in Australia: More Walkers and Bicyclists, Safer Walking and Bicycling," *Health Promotion Journal of Australia* 16 (2005), 47-51.

12. Willard, *How I Learned to Ride the Bicycle,* 67.

13. John Forester, *Effective Cycling* (Cambridge: MIT Press, 1984).

14. "San Francisco's Shared Lane Pavement Markings: Improving Bicycle Safety," February 2004, a final report prepared by Alta Planning and Design for the San Francisco Department of Parking and Traffic.

15. Dawn Royal and Darby Miller-Steiger, "National Survey of Bicyclist and Pedestrian Attitudes and Behavior," Report prepared for National Highway Traffic Safety Administration, 2008. Note this report uses 2002 data.

16. National Bicycle Dealers' Association statistics.

17. "Grand Exhibit of Bicycles," *New York Times*, 7 January 1894.

18. Phred Dvorak, "San Francisco Ponders: Could Bike Lanes Cause Pollution?" *Wall Street Journal*, 20 August 2008.

19. The stations in question were WMJI in Cleveland, WDCG in Raleigh, and KLOL in Houston. "Bicyclists Take On Radio Empire," cnn.com, 1 November 2003. www.cnn.com/2003/US/Midwest/11/01/radio.bicyclists.ap/.

20. This is my interpretation of the basis of Forester's philosophy as far as it is explicated in Forester, *Effective Cycling*.

This interpretation has been disputed by self-described Vehicular Cyclists but not effectively enough to dislodge me from it.

21. "Bicyclist Fatalities and Serious Injuries in New York City, 1996-2005." A joint report from the New York City Department of Health and Mental Hygiene, Parks and Recreation, Transportation and the New York City Police Department, 28.

22. Kenneth Cross, "Identifying Critical Behavior Leading to Collisions between Bicycles and Motor Vehicles," presented to the California Statewide Bicycle Committee, 1974. www.johnforester.com/Articles/Safety/Cross01.htm. This article shows clearly that younger riders tend to have different types of collisions than adults and are much more likely to be found legally at fault than are adult riders.

23. Insurance Institute for Highway Safety. www.iihs.org/research/fatality_facts_2006/bicycles.html.

24. "Injury to Pedestrians and Bicyclists: An Analysis Based on Hospital Emergency Department Data," Federal Highway Administration, gives some sense of the raw numbers of bicyclists injured in collisions with motor vehicles, and of the way studies based on police reports badly underestimate the total number of bicyclist emergency room visits. See also Halleyesus, Annest, and Dellinger, "Cyclists Injured while Sharing the Road with Motor Vehicles," *Injury Prevention*, June 2007, 202-6. Determining the portion of these injured who were riding lawfully when struck is an inexact exercise, but rough estimates can be deduced from various sources, including

"Bicyclist Fatalities and Serious Injuries in New York City, 1996-2005." A joint report from the New York City Department of Health and Mental Hygiene, Parks and Recreation, Transportation and the New York City Police Department, 28. For the specific look-but-failed-to-see phenomenon, see Mai-Britt Herslund and Niels Jorgenson, "Looked-but-Failed-to-See-Errors in Traffic," *Accident Analysis and Prevention* 35 (November 2003): 885-91. Ivan Brown, "Review of the 'Looked but Failed to See' Accident Causation Factor," Department for Transport, London, November 2005. B. L. Hills, "Vision, Visibility and Perception in Driving," *Perception* (1980): 183-216. Hill notes: "There is now much evidence that the driver is quite often operating beyond his visual or perceptual capabilities in a number of key driving situations." Yeah, s/he is.

25. "Saved from Potter's Field," *New York Times*, 27 May 1893. The title of the article refers to the paupers' cemetery, not Isaac Potter.

26. Robert Mitchum, "City to Step Up Enforcement of Bike Laws," *Chicago Tribune*, 22 August 2008. Meanwhile, the Idaho statute (http://itd.idaho.gov/bike_ped/) reads:

49-720. STOPPING — TURN AND STOP SIGNALS. (1) A person operating a bicycle or human-powered vehicle approaching a stop sign shall slow down and, if required for safety, stop before entering the intersection. After slowing to a reasonable speed or stopping, the person shall yield the right-of-way to any vehicle in the intersection or approaching on another highway so closely as to constitute an immediate hazard during the time the person is moving across or within the intersection or junction of highways, except that a person after slowing to a reasonable speed and yielding the right-of-way if required, may cautiously make a turn or proceed through the intersection without stopping. (2) A person operating a bicycle or human-powered vehicle approaching a steady red traffic control light shall stop before entering the intersection and shall yield to all other traffic. Once the person has yielded, he may proceed through the steady red light with caution. Provided however, that a person after slowing to a reasonable speed and yielding the right-of-way if required, may cautiously make a right-hand turn. A left-hand turn onto a one-way highway may be made on a red light after stopping and yielding to other traffic.

VII: The Sorry State of the Motoring Dream

1. Henry Ford, *Today and Tomorrow* (New York: Doubleday, Page and Company, 1926), 165.
2. Hiram Maxim, *Horseless Carriage Days* (New York: Harper and Brothers, 1936), 8.
3. Cutler Cleveland, "On Energy Transitions Past and Future," 28 December 2007. www.theoildrum.com/node/3442.
4. "911 Callers Looking for Gas in Metro Atlanta Jam Emergency Phone Lines," WSBTV.com, 28 September 2008. www.wsbtv.com/news/17575718/detail.html.

5. "Drivers Angry at Atlanta Gas Shortages," WGCL Atlanta, 22 September 2008. www.cbs46.com/news/17526456/detail.html#-. "Local Gas Shortage Just a Symptom of a Long-Term Problem," 24 September 2008. www.citizen-times.com/apps/pbcs.dll/article?AID=200880923042.

6. U.S. Department of Energy's Standby Gasoline Rationing Plan, February 1979. The DOE outline of the plan states: "…The plan provides that eligibility for ration allotments will be primarily on the basis of motor vehicle registrations. DOE will mail government ration checks to the parties named in a national vehicle registration file to be maintained by DOE. Ration recipients may cash these checks for ration coupons at various designated coupon issuance points. Retail outlets and other suppliers will be required to redeem the ration coupons received in exchange for gasoline sold. Supplemental gas will be given to high-priority activities. A ration banking system will be established with two separate and distinct types of ration accounts: Retail outlets and other suppliers will open redemption accounts for the deposit of redeemed ration rights; and individuals or firms may open ration rights accounts, which will operate in much the same manner as monetary checking accounts. A white market will be permitted for the sale of transfer of ration rights…" www.osti.gov/energycitations/product.biblio.jsp?osti_id=6307185.

7. Shawn Tully, "Why Oil Prices Will Tank," cnnmoney.com, 6 June 2008. http://money.cnn.com/2008/06/06/news/economy/tully_oil_bust.fortune.

8. Interim Report on Crude Oil, Interagency Task Force on the Commodities Markets, Commodities Futures Trading Commission, July 2008. David Cho, "A Few Speculators Dominate Vast Market For Oil Trading," *Washington Post*, 21 August 2008, 1.
9. Matthew Simmons, *Twilight in the Desert* (Hoboken, N.J.: John Wiley and Sons, 2005), 286.
10. Production rates were controlled through the Texas Railroad Commission. www.rrc.state.tx.us/about/history/.
11. Simmons, *Twilight in the Desert*, 286-97.
12. Eric Watkins, "Pemex Annual Oil Output Slides 10%; Cantarell 36%," *Oil & Gas Journal*, 23 August 2008. www.ogj.com.
13. Government Accountability Office, "Crude Oil: Uncertainty about Future Oil Supply Makes It Important to Develop a Strategy for Addressing a Peak and Decline in Oil Production," 2007, 12.
14. Tom Hamburger and Alan Miller, "Halliburton's Interests Assisted by White House," *Los Angeles Times*, 14 October 2004.
15. For instance, R. M. Morse and D. K. Flavin, "The Definition of Alcoholism," *JAMA* 268, no. 8 (26 August 1992): 1012-14. There is no single definition of addiction but across different fields the definition tends to include continued use of a substance despite adverse consequences, and denial.
16. Arthur Goldschmidt Jr., *A Concise History of the Middle East* (Boulder: Westview Press, 1983), 302-3.
17. Simmons, *Twilight in the Desert*, 33-67.

18. Ibid., 63-67. Simmons notes that due to the peculiar geology of oil reservoirs, the multiple forced production spikes from Saudi Arabia could very well have damaged their ability to produce over the long term.

19. Justin Lahart, *The Australian*, 26 March 2008. www .theaustralian.news.au/story/o,25197,23431099 28737,00.html. The IEA's projection for global oil demand in 2030 is 106 million barrels-per-day, which has been revised downward by 10 million barrels-per-day since last year's estimate. www.iea.org/Textbase/npsum/ WEO2008SUM.pdf.

20. Quoted in Thomas Friedman, "Flush with Energy," *New York Times*, 10 August 2008.

21. Jonathan Martin and Chris Frates, "Novak Cited after Hitting Pedestrian," politico.com, 23 July 2008. The reporters happened to be walking by at the time. Novak said he thought Bono was a bike messenger. In fact, Bono was a partner at a well-known Washington law firm.

22. "National Pedestrian Crash Report," National Highway Traffic Safety Administration, June 2008.

23. Robert Novak, "Mission to Niger," *Washington Post*, 14 July 2003, 21.

24. Novak told his side of the story in a column: "How a Tumor Is Changing My Life," *Washington Post*, 6 September 2008.

25. "Takes Issue with Hill," *New York Times*, 5 June 1910.

26. Nick Snow, "API: US Oil Demand Dropped 3% during First Half of 2008," *Oil & Gas Journal*, 18 July 2008.

27. "Diesel Usage up by 35%," *Times of India*, 23 August 2008. http://timesofindia.indiatimes.com/Chennai/Diesel_usage_up_by_35/articleshow/3395003.cms.

28. Jan Wong, *Jan Wong's China* (Toronto: Doubleday Canada, 1999), 212.

29. Ariana Eunjung Cha, "China's Cars Accelerating Global Demand for Fuel," *Washington Post*, 8 July 2008, 1.

30. Justin Lahart and Conor Dougherty, "U.S. Retools Economy, Curbing Thirst for Oil," *Wall Street Journal*, 12 August 2008, 18.

31. Hitler's explanation to a *Detroit News* interviewer in 1931 when asked why there was a large oil painting of Henry Ford hanging over his desk.

32. Nick Bunkley, "An S.U.V. Traffic Jam," *New York Times*, 12 August 2008, Business section.

33. Kenneth Jackson, *Crabgrass Frontier* (New York: Oxford University Press, 1985), 170. Jackson writes: "By 1950, General Motors had been involved in the replacement of more than one hundred streetcar operations—including those of Los Angeles, St. Louis, Philadelphia, Baltimore and Salt Lake City—with GM-manufactured buses. A federal grand jury ultimately found the giant corporation guilty of criminal conspiracy, but the total fine—$5,000—was less than the profit returned for the conversion of a single streetcar."

34. Michael Dobbs, "Ford and GM Scrutinized for Alleged Nazi Collaboration; Firms Deny Claims on Aiding German War Effort," *Washington Post*, 30 November 1998.

35. Christopher Conkey, "Funds for Highways Plummet as Drivers Cut Gasoline Use," *Wall Street Journal*, 28 July 2008, 1.

36. Ben Oliver, "Oil Warrior: Former CIA Chief James Woolsey Says If You Want to Beat Bin Laden, Buy a Prius," *Motor Trend*. www.motortrend.com/features/112_0705_james_woolsey_interview/index.html.

37. Energy Information Administration, "U.S. Petroleum Balance Sheet, 4 Weeks Ending 10/31/08." www.eia.doe.gov/pub/oil_gas/petroleum/data_publications/weekly_petroleum_status_report/current/txt/table1.txt. Page is updated regularly. It should be noted that a substantial portion of this imported oil is piped down from Canada.

38. In a 2007 report called "Dust to Dust: The Energy Costs of New Vehicles from Concept to Disposal," CNW Marketing Research, Inc. claimed to show that if a Prius is driven relatively sparingly and travels only about one hundred thousand miles in its lifetime, it could end up with a higher per-mile energy cost than a Hummer, Cadillac Escalade, or similar beast. www.cnwmr.com/nss-folder/automotiveenergy/. The report's methodology remained a mystery and it was loudly condemned from several corners. For instance, see Peter Gleick, "Hummer versus Prius: Dust to Dust Report Misleads the Media and Public with Bad Science," Pacific Institute, May 2007. www.pacinst.org/topics/integrity_of_science/case_studies/hummer_versus_prius.html.

39. According to the Energy Information Administration, about 70 percent of electricity generated in the United

States in 2006 originated from a natural gas or coal plant. Coal's share is slowly but steadily coming down, also according to the EIA.

40. Ulf Bossel, "Does a Hydrogen Economy Make Sense?" *Proceedings of the IEEE*, vol. 94, no. 10, October 2006, 1826.

VIII: Reasons to Ride

1. Fred Kelly, *The Wright Brothers* (New York: Harcourt, Brace and Company, 1943), 38.
2. James Tobin, *To Conquer the Air* (New York: Simon and Schuster, 2004), 53. Stephen Kirk, *First in Flight* (Winston-Salem: Blair, 1995), 22.
3. "Automobile Topics of Interest," *New York Times*, 5 October 1902.
4. Hiram Maxim, *Horseless Carriage Days* (New York: Harper and Brothers, 1936), 175.
5. Interview with Cal Marsella, director of the Regional Transportation District, *PBS Newshour*, 20 June 2008.
6. Paul Dudley White, *My Life and Medicine: An Autobiographical Memoir* (Boston: Gambit, 1971), 223.
7. Mayer Hillman, "Cycling and the Promotion of Health," 1992.
8. W. Tuxworth, A. M. Nevill, C. White, and C. Jenkins, "Health, Fitness, Physical Activity and Morbidity of Middle-Aged Factory Workers," *British Journal of Industrial Medicine* 43, no. 11 (November 1986): 733-75.
9. For instance, see N. Orsini, C. S. Mantzoros, and A. Wolk, "Association of Physical Activity with Cancer

Incidence, Mortality, and Survival: A Population-Based Study of Men," *British Journal of Cancer* 98, no. 11 (3 June 2008): 1864-69. The researchers followed more than forty thousand Swedish men aged forty-five to seventy-nine for six years and found a "strong inverse linear association" between activity levels and cancer incidence and morbidity.

10. White, *My Life and Medicine*, 214-25.
11. David Gordon Wilson, *Bicycling Science* (Cambridge: MIT Press, 2004), 153-61.
12. Ibid., 162.

BIBLIOGRAPHY

Allen, John. *Street Smarts*. Emmaus, Pa.: Rodale Press, 1988.

Berto, Frank, Ron Shephard, and Raymond Henry, *The Dancing Chain*. San Francisco: Van der Plas, 2000.

Bierce, Ambrose. *The Devil's Dictionary*. New York: Neale Publishing Company, 1911; Mineola, N.Y.: Dover Publications, 1993.

Doyle, Jack. *Taken for a Ride*. New York: Four Walls Eight Windows, 2000.

Dzierzak, Lou. *The Evolution of American Bicycle Racing*. Guilford, Conn.: Globe Pequot Press, 2007.

Epperson, Bruce. "Failed Colossus: Strategic Error at the Pope Manufacturing Company," *Technology and Culture* 41, no. 2 (April 2000): 300-20.

Fall, Bernard. *Hell in a Very Small Place*. Philadelphia: Da Capo Press, 1966.

Ferguson, Niall. War of the World: *Twentieth-Century Conflict and the Descent of the West*. New York: Penguin Books, 2006.

Fitzpatrick, Jim. *The Bicycle in Wartime: An Illustrated History*. Washington: Brassey's, 1998.

Flink, James. *The Automobile Age*. Cambridge: MIT Press, 1988.

Ford, Bryan. *Clara: Mrs. Henry Ford*. Detroit: Wayne State University Press, 2002.

Ford, Henry. *My Life and Work*. New York: Doubleday, Page and Sons, 1922.

———. *Today and Tomorrow*. New York: Doubleday, Page and Company, 1926.

Forester, John. *Bicycle Transportation: A Handbook for Cycling Transportation Engineers*. Cambridge: MIT Press, 1994.

———. *Effective Cycling*. Cambridge: MIT Press, 1984.

Garreau, Joel. *Edge City*. New York: Doubleday, 1991.

Gillett, Charlie. *The Sound of the City*. New York: Pantheon Books, 1983.

Glover, Edwin Maurice. *In 70 Days: The Story of the Japanese Campaign in British Malaya*. London: Frederick Muller Limited, 1946.

Goldschmidt, Arthur, Jr., *A Concise History of the Middle East*. Boulder: Westview Press, 1983. Heilbronner, Robert. *An Inquiry into the Human Prospect: Updated and Reconsidered for the 1980s*. New York: W. W. Norton and Company, 1980.

Heinberg, Richard. *The Party's Over: Oil, War and the Fate of Industrial Societies*. Gabriola Island, British Columbia: New Society Publishers, 2003.

Hughes, Thomas. *American Genesis: A Century of Invention and Technological Enthusiasm, 1870-1970*. Chicago: University of Chicago Press, 2004.

Hurst, Robert. *The Art of Cycling*. Guilford, Conn.: Globe Pequot Press, 2007. This book was previously published as *The Art of Urban Cycling*, 2004.

Ingham, John. *Biographical Dictionary of American Business Leaders*. Westport, Conn.: Greenwood Publishing Group, 1983.

Jackson, Kenneth. *Crabgrass Frontier*. New York: Oxford University Press, 1985.

Jacobs, Jane. *The Death and Life of Great American Cities*. New York: Random House, 1961.

Kelly, Fred. *The Wright Brothers*. New York: Harcourt, Brace and Company, 1943.

Kirby, Major-General S. Woodburn, *Singapore: The Chain of Disaster*. New York: Macmillan Company, 1971.

Kirk, Stephen. *First in Flight*. Winston-Salem: Blair, 1995.

Kunstler, James Howard. *The City in Mind: Meditations on the Urban Condition*. New York: Free Press, 2001.

———. *Geography of Nowhere*. New York: Simon and Schuster, 1993.

———. *The Long Emergency*. New York: The Atlantic Monthly Press, 2005.

Maxim, Hiram Percy. *Horseless Carriage Days*. New York: Harper and Brothers, 1936.

Mionske, Bob. *Bicycling and the Law*. Boulder: Velo Press, 2007.

Nye, Peter. *Hearts of Lions*. New York: W. W. Norton and Company, 1988.

Rae, John. *American Automobile Manufacturers*. Philadelphia: Chilton and Company, 1959.

———. *The Road and the Car in American Life*. Cambridge: MIT Press, 1971.

Ritchie, Andrew. *Major Taylor: The Extraordinary Career of a Champion Bicycle Racer*. Baltimore: Johns Hopkins University Press, 1996.

Sharp, Archibald. *Bicycles and Tricycles: An Elementary Treatise on Their Design and Construction.* London: Longmans, Green and Company, 1896.

Simmons, Matthew. *Twilight in the Desert.* Hoboken, N.J.: John Wiley and Sons, 2005.

Smith, Robert. *A Social History of the Bicycle.* New York: American Heritage Press, 1972.

Tainter, Joseph. *The Collapse of Complex Societies.* Cambridge: Cambridge University Press, 1990.

Taylor, Marshall. *The Fastest Bicycle Rider in the World: The Story of a Colored Boy's Indomitable Courage and Success against Great Odds.* Worcester: Wormley Publishing, 1928.

Tsuji, Masanobu. *Japan's Greatest Victory, Britain's Worst Defeat.* Translated by Margaret Lake. New York: Da Capo Press, 1997.

Vanderbilt, Tom. *Traffic: Why We Drive the Way We Do (and What It Says about Us).* New York: Alfred A. Knopf, 2008.

White, Paul Dudley. *My Life and Medicine: An Autobiographical Memoir.* Boston: Gambit, 1971.

Willard, Frances. *How I Learned to Ride the Bicycle: Reflections of an Influential 19th Century Woman.* Sunnyvale, Calif.: Fair Oaks Publishing, 1991. Originally published as *Wheel within a Wheel,* 1895.

Wilson, David Gordon. *Bicycling Science.* Cambridge: MIT Press, 2004.

INDEX

accidents. *See* fatalities; injuries
ACRA (American Cycle Racing
  Association), 38
activism, 61–64
ADC (American Dream Coalition), 91
adventure, 138, 169–71
advocacy
  European models and, 134–37
  in history, 13–14, 15, 16
  safety and, 80, 88
  Vehicular Cyclists, 89–90
aerodynamics, and clothing, 74–75
African American bicycle racers, 31, 34–42,
  48–49
Agassi, Shai, 25
airplanes, 167–68, 170
American Cycle Racing Association
  (ACRA), 38
American Dream Coalition (ADC), 91
Anderson, Rob, 101
Anthony, Susan B., 28
anti-bicyclist sentiment, 99–102
Arab-Israeli War, 68, 130
Arrow (race car), 44
arson, 22–24
Atlanta, Georgia, 117–18
automobile industry
  bailout loans, 151, 152, 155–56
  bankruptcy ramifications, 156–57
  failure of, 150–52, 155, 157
  inventors as former bicycle
    manufacturers, 10, 13, 14, 19

SUV popularity, 150
US government promotion of, in
  history, 152–55
during World War II, 153–54
automobiles. *See also* motoring; motorists
  bicycle collisions with, 82–83,
    85–86, 104, 105–6
  bicycle industry influencing
    development of, 10, 18
  China and increase sales of, 144
  cost of, compared to bicycles, 26
  development of, and decline in
    cycling, 14, 42
  electric, history of, 25
  energy efficiency of, 177–78
  Ford's first, description of, 19–20
  future visions of, 5
  history of gasoline-powered, 8–11,
    12, 17–18, 19–20, 170
  hybrids, 157–61, 163, 177–78
  India and increase sales of, 143–44
  pedestrian accidents with, 139–40
  petroleum consumption of, 2
  racing (*see* racing, automobile)
awareness, 103–4, 108

Baby Bullet (race car), 47
Bacon, Kevin, 71
Bald, Eddie "Cannon," 39
Barnes Dance, 111
Barron, Hugh J., 52–53
Becker, W. E., 37

chafing, 75
"Chainguard" discussion group, 29
chauffeur, term origins, 46
Chicago, Illinois, 110, 111
children
     bicycle-car collisions involving, 105
     bicycling fatalities involving, 84,
          86–87
     teenage drivers, 146–50
China, 55–57, 143, 144, 145
Chrysler, 155–57
class-consciousness (elitism), 28–29, 31
Clear Channel Communications, 101–2
Cleveland, Cutler, 115
clothing and accessories
     in history, 69–74
     as obstacle to bicycles as everyday
          transportation, 75
     practical benefits of, 74–75
     promoting anti-bicyclist sentiment,
          100
     psychology of, 32, 74
CNN, 101
Code of Movement, 107–9
collisions
     automobile, as teenage rite of
          passage, 148
     automobile-bicycle, 82–83, 85–86,
          104, 105–6, 141–42
     automobile-pedestrians, 139–40
combat bicycles, 53–54, 58–61
Commodities Futures Trading Commission
     (CFTC), 120
commuters, 86, 87
ConocoPhillips, 132
conservative vs. liberal, 98
Cooper, Tom
     automobile racing, 42–47
     bicycle racing, 38–40, 41–45
     death of, 47–48
Copenhagen, Denmark, 134
couriers (messengers), 52, 103
crimes committed on bicycles, 15
Critical Mass rides, 61–64

cycling advocacy organizations, 13
cyclists
     bad behaviors of, 100
     children as, 84, 86–87, 105
     energy efficiency of, 176–78
     harassment and violence toward,
          101–2
     ideological conflicts between, 29
     intolerance of, 31–32
     North Korean restrictions on, 26–27
     novice, and perception of traffic,
          103–4
     resentment toward motorists, 100
     responsibility of, 88
     terminology, 29

Daimler, 156
danger. See also fatalities; injuries
     benefits outweighing risks of, 175
     fear and perception of, 79–80
     vulnerability to, 141
Dave Stohler (movie character), 70–71
Davis, Jefferson, 24
deaths. See fatalities
Democratic National Conventions,
     62–63, 65
demonstrations, 62–63, 65
Denmark, 25, 134
Denver, Colorado, 94–95, 110, 111, 136,
     172–73
Department of Commerce, 5
dernies, 38
discrimination, 14, 28, 30–31, 34, 35–37
dooring collisions, 105
drivers, automobile. See motorists
driving. See motoring
Duryea brothers, 10
Dutch, 55

Eck, Tom, 40
Eisenhower, Dwight D. "Ike," 153, 154
electricity, 163, 164
electric vehicles
     history of, 25

"Hill, the" (Boulder, Colorado), 21
Hillman, Mayer, 175
hit-and-run collisions, 139–40, 141–42
Hitler, Adolph, 150, 154, 157
Holland, 55
hoodlums, 15
horse-drawn carriages, 15, 17–18
horse-less carriages, 13, 170. *See also*
    automobiles
Huff, Ed "Spider," 44
hurricanes, and oil refinery damage, 116
hybrid-electric vehicles (HEVs), 157–61,
    177–78
hybrid vehicles, plug-in, 163, 178
hydrocarbons, liquid, 22–23
hydrogen, 164

Idaho, 109–10
India, 143–44
injuries
    in automobile racing, 47
    bicycle-car collisions, 82–83, 85, 104,
        105–6
    bicyclist's responsibility and, 88,
        104–6
    causes of, 82
    child cyclists and, 86
    child drivers and, 148
    compared to driving, 81
    messengers and, 103
    as risk, 175
    statistics, 82
    types of, 83
    wobbliness *vs.* skill, 77–78
Insurance Institute for Highway Safety, 148
International Energy Agency, 132
inventor, defined, 19
Iran, 130–31
Iraq, 131–32
Israel, 25

Jacobsen, Peter, 85–86, 88
Jacquelin, Edmund, 41
Japan, 57–60, 145

Japanese keirin racing, 38
Japanese troops, 58–61
jerseys, 70, 75
Jones, Earl, 30–31
Junior, Dale, 38, 141

Keifer, Eddie, 21, 22
keragen, 125–26
Kifer, Ken, 81
Kim Jong II, 26–27
King, Charles, 10, 19
Kiser, Earl, 47
Kleinschmidt, Edward, 15
Klondike Bicycle, 52
KTSE (radio station), 102
Kundera, Milan, 55
Kuwait, 131–32

Lantenberg, David, 41
LAW. *See* League of American Wheelmen
    (LAW)
law enforcement, 16, 51, 109–11
lawfulness, 103–4, 106, 107–11
Lawson, Iver, 41, 42
lawsuits against bicyclists, 101
League of American Wheelmen (LAW)
    accident statistics, 81
    creation of, 13
    early bicycling advocacy, 13–14
    Forester and, 91
    membership and racism, 30–31
    membership profile, early, 28
    members of, 169–70
legislation
    bicycle registration and licensing, 15
    cyclist usage of roadways, 14
    public park access, 14
    road access and traffic rules, 90
    road improvements, 13–14
    traffic codes and, 109–10
    train access, 14
    transportation classification of
        bicycles, 15–17
Levick, Virginia, 48

United Kingdom, 123
United States
    automobile-population ratios, 144
    oil consumption of, 2, 143, 145,
       158–60
    oil dependency development of, 130,
       152–55, 158
    oil embargoes on, 130
    oil supply perceptions of, 114–15,
       119–20
    promotion of automobile industry,
       152–55
United States Military Wheelmen, 52–53

vehicles, motor. *See* automobiles; motoring;
    motorists
Vehicular Cycling, 89–90, 103
velodromes (bike track racing), 38
violence toward cyclists, 101–2
Vitol, 120
vulnerability, 141, 148

Wall Street Journal, 101
Walther pneumatic, 21
Ward, Maria, 26
wartime uses of bicycles, 52–54, 58–60
Watts, W. W., 30
wheelmen (early bicyclists)
    clothing worn by, 70
    as cycling advocates, 13–14, 15–16
    early conflict and distrust between,
       15, 29
    as motor vehicle gapers, 17, 18
    negative public perceptions of,
       15–16, 29
    nineteenth century profiles of, 28–29,
       31–32
    racism and, 30
    terminology, 29
    women as, 27–28, 70, 73

Wheel within a Wheel (Willard), 73
White, Paul Dudley, 174, 175
Willard, Frances, 73, 77–78, 89
Williams, Bull, 41
Wills, Harold, 44
Wilson, Charles, 153, 154
Winton, Alexander, 10, 42, 47
women
    as bicycle promoters, 73
    bicycling clothing worn by, 70, 73
    cycling as symbol of liberation for,
       27, 28
    cycling restrictions in North Korea
       for, 26–27
    as endurance bicyclists, 27–28
    nineteenth century attitudes toward,
       27–28
Women's Christian Temperance Union, 73
Woolsey, James, 157, 163
World War II, 60–61, 79–80, 153–54
Wright, Orville, 167–68
Wright, Wilbur, 167–68

Zimmerman, Arthur, 35

ABOUT THE AUTHOR

Robert Hurst is a veteran bicycle messenger and all-around urban cyclist who has cycled more than 15,000 hours in heavy traffic and completed more than 80,000 deliveries. Hurst is also the author of *Mountain Biking Colorado's San Juan Mountains: Durango and Telluride, Road Biking Colorado's Front Range,* and *The Art of Cycling: A Guide to Bicycling in 21st-Century America* (all FalconGuides).